MW00715115

TOM LONGBOAT

Running Against the Wind

A First Nations Canadian
Conquers the World's Marathons

BIBLIOTHÈQUE SAINT-CLAUDE LIBRARY
C. P. 200
SAINT-CLAUDE, MANITOBA R0G 1Z0 379-2524

WILL CARDINAL

ESCHIA
BOOKS

Contents

Dedication

To all Aboriginal athletes who paved the way
for future generations, and to the great
Tom Longboat for simply doing what he did best.

DO NOT TAPE OR REPAIR LIBRARY BOOKS

Acknowledgements

I would personally like to thank Tom Longboat. In a time and place when the world thought of his people as less than, Tom Longboat, Cogwagee, by sheer force of talent, determination and courage, showed the world that his people were strong, that his people were noble, and that his people could rise to the top.

Introduction

Out of childhood into manhood,
Now had grown my Hiawatha,
Skilled in the craft of hunters,
Learned in all the lore of old men.
In all youthful sports and pastimes,
In all manly arts and labors,
Swift of foot was Hiawatha.
He could shoot an arrow from him,
And run forward with such fleetness,
That the arrow fell behind him.

– Henry Wadsworth Longfellow

It is early spring 1905, and a young 17-year-old Tom Longboat is about to take the field for his Onondaga Nation lacrosse team for a regular-season Six Nations league game, in a windswept park in southwest Ontario. He looks around the field and watches the crowds gathering around the sidelines. A few are arguing over the outcome of the game and others are lost in conversation, but he notices a majority of the eyes are staring in his direction.

"Hey, Tom, score one for me!" yells one fan.

"Faster than lightning, Tom!" cheers another.

He knows people are expecting a lot from him, but the 17-year-old is remarkably confident. He closes his eyes and listens to the crowd, waiting for his chance to show them what he can do. At the sound of the referee's whistle, Longboat grabs his stick and hits the grass running.

The game is about to begin, and the stands and sidelines are packed to capacity with eager fans. A huge cheer goes up as the crowd catches sight of Longboat. He breathes into his hands and watches the hot air from his lungs hit the cold air in a puff.

The referee signals to both teams, and with a piercing blow of his whistle the game is underway. Longboat springs into action and begins to run around the field. The opponent assigned to cover him can barely keep up, and in what seems like an instant, a teammate spots Tom out in the open and feeds him a pass as he is in mid-stride headed in on the opposing goaltender. In the blink of an eye, Tom crosses the length of the field and puts the ball behind a shell-shocked goaltender for the score.

For not one second did Longboat stop running during that game, and when the final whistle sounded, the Onondaga Nation had won. The crowd filed out of the stadium well satisfied at having watched one of the fastest players in recent history, and the frantic discussions began anew as to what Longboat would do in his next game.

After the game, while Tom and his teammates were celebrating the win, he noticed one of the players was not looking particularly happy. It seemed this player was a little jealous of all the attention being paid to Tom, and wanting to prove his worth, he stood up in front of all the other teammates and right there challenged Tom to a race. Tom had been running since he was a little kid but had never raced anyone in a competition before, but he decided to accept his teammate's challenge.

The next day the two runners met along the side of one of the reserve's roads, with the rest of their teammates there to cheer them on. Looking back on that day years later, Longboat could not remember the distance they ran, but all that really mattered was that he left his challenger in his dust trail. From the moment they started the race, Longboat was out in front of his challenger, and he never looked back. The race itself was insignificant, and he took no pleasure in embarrassing his teammate, but the race intrigued Tom who then thought that he could use his natural speed and endurance on the competitive circuit. A few weeks later, Longboat decided to try his luck in the Victoria Day race, a five-mile run in the neighbouring town of Caledonia, Ontario.

It was the tradition in those days to celebrate Queen Victoria's birthday by throwing a fair with games, concession stands, as well as the feature attraction of a hotly anticipated running race of the local young men, both white and Native.

People flooded in from the surrounding towns for the fair wearing their Sunday best. It was the time of year to catch up with old friends and to socialize, but mostly to gather to watch the annual foot race. Older men placed bets on a winner, and the young women got to take a look at the young healthy men.

Although no socializing usually took place between the whites and the Natives at that time, during the competition all barriers came down; it was considered a race of endurance and strength and not of colour or class. This idea appealed to Tom because he and his people had spent their lives on the edges of society. He realized that despite the colour of his skin, he would be able taste the freedom of belonging for at least one glorious moment when he crossed the line in first place.

All activity at the fair suddenly came to a halt just before the race was set to start. Tom gathered in the crowd of other racers and resolved to start the race with the same energy he had when he had destroyed his teammate on the road back at the reserve.

At the sound of the gun he shot off the line at top speed and did not let up once. Fans gathered on the side of the road could not believe their eyes as this young Native fellow came out of nowhere and challenged the well-known runners of the towns. However, these runners had experience and knew how to pace themselves for the miles ahead. Longboat, though filled with the energy and arrogance of youth, had no strategy, and by the fifth mile of the race he gave up the lead to one runner.

Longboat managed to hang on to take second place, but rather than being disappointed in his results, the ease with which he finished at the top spurred him to want to race again. Certainly those in attendance were captivated by his performance and rallied around him after the race to encourage him to enter other races.

But Longboat did not need any encouragement. He ran for the sheer pleasure of running, and he ran in his own way. Some Native runners employed a different method when it came to a race. While white runners would often rest the day before a race, it was not uncommon for Longboat to stay up all night. Running was not simply the pursuit to be the fastest, it was a spiritual escape for the traditional Native runner.

Running gave Longboat a feeling of freedom. It was the call to feel the wind hitting his face, the sound of his footfalls, and the sensation of his legs moving him along a path. Running cleared his mind and let him escape the worries of the day, and for a young Native at the turn of the 20th century, it was all he could do to leave the grim existence of the reserve behind. But to achieve that he had to run very far.

Chapter One

Mercury Rising

THE PEOPLE OF THE SIX NATIONS once lived in freedom and relative peace. Living in the areas just south of the St. Lawrence River and near the Great Lakes, the tribes of the Six Nations—the Onondaga, Mohawk, Oneida, Seneca, Cayuga and Tuscarora—had farmed the fertile soils and hunted in the thick forest for hundreds of years. With the arrival of the white man from Europe, the Aboriginal way of life did not change immediately. The tribes saw the Europeans as another partner to trade with and barter for goods. At first it was a prosperous union of cultures as the Europeans were providing metal tools, weapons and animals that they had never seen, and the Native people in return provided the white man with furs and guides to show them how to survive in these new lands. But as time went on, it became apparent that the white men wanted more than only trading partners. It was land they were after, and the people of the Six Nations were living on the best property.

Acre by acre the lands of the Six Nations were slowly taken over by the government, and a once free and proud people were confined to tracks of land that were referred to as reserves. Without land and the freedom to move about, the tribe's traditions began dying off with each generation, and the young were forced to integrate into the emerging world of North America.

Although many traditions died off with older generations, others continued to flourish. Sport or athletics had always been a part of aboriginal life, and at the dusk of the 19th century, Native people were considered to be some of the greatest athletes. Jim Thorpe probably remains the most famous Native athlete of all time. He truly was a renaissance man when it came to sport. He was a track and field star, he played professional football, professional baseball, was an Olympic gold medallist, a lacrosse player—just about every sport on earth, Jim Thorpe played. But in one sport in particular, some skinny kid sprinting around the reserve began to grab people's attention.

In those days, the foot race was the most popular sporting event of its time. Organized team sports had yet to take a foothold in the greater society at large as they do today. Since most people lived in isolated rural areas and worked off the land, they didn't have much opportunity to get together for games, but when it came time for the yearly fair or community celebrations, foot races were the feature of the day. The young men showed off their skills while the older men bet money on the runners.

Although largely marginalized by society, Native people were welcome to compete in these races, and despite their small numbers in comparison to the whites, the Native runners were usually the ones most people bet their money on. It wasn't that Aboriginal people possessed some sort of natural physical advantage over their white counterparts; athletics in general had always been a part of Native culture. Many of the early Native running specialists had played the cardio-intensive game of lacrosse in the summer and were quite adept snowshoe runners in the winter, making the transition to the racetrack nearly seamless.

One of the most successful early Native runners, a man that paved the way for people like Tom Longboat, was Lewis Bennett, or was he was more commonly called, Deerfoot. A Seneca from the Cattaraugus Reservation, Lewis Bennett began running for the sheer pleasure of it in the confines of his reserve. He had never really given any thought to running in a competition, but one day at the age of 26, he decided to test his skills against others at the 1856 Erie County fair. The race was set at five miles, something he had done with his eyes closed on the reserve but never up against any competitors. It was not much of a challenge for Lewis as he completed the five-mile course in 25 minutes and took home the top prize of $50. He not only managed to win the race but his coming-out-of-nowhere story also seemed to capture the public's imagination. The story of his incredible win hit the newspapers, and soon he was receiving invitations to participate in races all across Canada, the United States and even Great Britain.

Apart from his natural running talent, the public was attracted to the entertainment aspect that Bennett brought to the racetrack. He had a sharp mind and knew at the time that if he did not capture the public's attention, another runner would come along and take over his spot. With a keen eye for self-promotion, Bennett changed his name to the fast-sounding "Deerfoot." The moniker was an obvious play to his Native heritage but it worked. With each passing race, more and more people came out to witness the speed of the man called Deerfoot.

Besides donning a new name, the six-foot, 160-pound Deerfoot also liked to race with a bare chest and occasionally wore a band with one eagle feather around his head. His dark skin as well as the war whoops he screamed when racing to victory also added to his mystique. This was the world of competitive racing at the time; a sport dominated by agents, betting establishments and promoters, and no one was more marketable than Deerfoot. He went along with the notion that many whites believed at the time—that an Aboriginal person was somehow better constructed for physical activity and possessed a natural advantage over his white counterparts. We may scoff at such ideas today, but the belief was widespread during Bennett's time, and Native athletes had to contend with it on a regular basis.

In the summer of 1861, an English promoter recognized the financial potential of getting an Aboriginal to compete on British soil and invited Bennett to participate in a series of races across the United Kingdom.

The British press swallowed the idea of their lads racing up against what they called "a genuine child of the prairie" and wanted to see who would be the victor. Bennett lost that first race in London in front of a crowd of more than 4000 spectators, but it was of no consequence because both the public and the press had fallen for the character of Deerfoot. Over the next 20 months Deerfoot toured throughout

Bibliotheque Saint-Claude Library

Europe, racing and challenging anyone who might pass his way. The intense competition helped him improve his running, and in the process he managed to set world records in the 10-mile and the 12-mile runs. (The actual times are not available.)

Deerfoot returned to North America to continue his running career, but eventually the passage of time slowed him down, and he stepped aside to allow the younger generations to take his place.

Despite the opening Deerfoot created for Aboriginal people in the running world, racist attitudes towards Native runners still existed. Dressing up runners in feathers and having them belt out war cries was bigoted enough in itself, but occasionally runners were often barred from races simply because of the colour of their skin.

In 1873 at a two-mile race in Montréal, a crowd took it into their hands to stop two Aboriginal runners from entering the event. The crowd was calmed down, and finally the two runners were allowed into the race, but when they finished first and second, the crowd got even angrier and nearly rioted.

Although this sort of animosity that resulted in a riot was a rare occurrence, the disconnect between the larger white community and the Aboriginals continued to grow. As the 19th century gave way to the 20th, the view of Native peoples began to sour for several reasons.

Between the late 1870s and into the early part of the 20th century, Native tribes were forced into less than favourable treaties with both the U.S. and Canadian governments, pushing them into marginalized lands. Forced to the margins of society, many Native communities had to rely on government assistance as a means of support. Because the people were confined to these small tracts of useless land, problems with alcoholism, drugs and violence began creeping into Native life. The attitude spread that Aboriginals were lazy and unwilling to learn the ways of "civilized" Christian society. This refusal to accept the new face of North American culture was seen as inferior, but in fact it was simply a rejection by most tribes to incorporate a system of values they did not consider important.

This prejudice followed Native athletes into every arena and still does somewhat to this day. But despite these obstacles, Native athletes were some of the most highly skilled at the time. But sport began to move away from the individual pursuit to team sports, and Aboriginal communities often did not have the population or the facilities to set up hockey or football leagues, and gradually the presence of Aboriginal people in professional sports declined. But a few top Native athletes were still around in the early 1900s, and one of the best was a young Canadian boy named Cogwagee, or more commonly known by his English name Tom Longboat.

The Six Nations Reserve where Longboat was born is located on the west bank of the Grand River just outside of the town of Brantford, Ontario. At one time the Six Nations land extended from the lower St. Lawrence River in the province of Québec into northeast United States along the Great Lakes. This territory got drastically smaller when during the American Revolution the Six Nations sided with the British, and in their defeat they were forced onto land that King George III gave them as a reward for their loyalty.

When the remaining people of the Six Nations settled onto the land, it stretched about 10 kilometres on both sides of the Grand River, but as time passed, the land was lost through fraudulent land sales, government projects and squatters. It was a place of gravel roads, high unemployment, poverty and had greater social problems than the rest of the North American population. It was into this community on June 4, 1887, that one Thomas Charles Longboat, or Cogwagee, was born.

Born to George and Betsy Longboat, Tom was the third of four children in the family household. His father supported the family by working the small piece of land surrounding their log cabin home, growing vegetables and raising a few farm animals.

It was a tough existence, and things got even worse for the family when the father died when Tom was just five years old.

Not having a father in the home was difficult for a family living off the land, and often the Longboat kids, including Tom who was not yet 10 years old, had to stay home from school to help his mother. But in between school and his chores, young Tom Longboat still had time to enjoy a little fun.

The discovery that he was a good runner came in an unusual manner. While out working in the fields all day in the vegetable garden and tending to the animals, Tom distracted himself from the tedium by chasing cows. It was fun at first, but when he caught up with the cows, he needed a new challenge. He eventually substituted the cows for his older brother, and soon the two were seen running all over the reserve. Tom knew little of what life was like off the reserve, but he got his introduction when some people from the Canadian government showed up at his home.

The Canadian government, in their infinite wisdom, had the idea that the Native population of the country needed to be rescued from their "heathen" lives and schooled in the ways of a proper Canadian. Generations of Native children were forcibly removed from their homes and placed in schools where they were punished for speaking their language and were not allowed home for long periods.

The church-run schools' intention was to give Native children an education, but often the experience was less than educational. Stories of abuse, both sexual and physical, were quite common, and many children upon leaving the schools lost the vital connection to their culture that they would have received on the reserve.

In the fall of 1899, 12-year-old Tom Longboat found himself in the same predicament as countless other Native children when he was sent to the Mohawk Institute, an Anglican mission school for Indians located in a rather idyllic location on the edge of Brantford, Ontario.

Walking down the long driveway, lined with trees and flower beds, Tom knew that this new school would not hold the promise of a good education that the government officials had told his mother it would. Upon walking into his first classes and getting read the rules, Tom knew that things were only going to get harder. He got to know the outside world through the priests and nuns who taught him, and with each passing day disliked his new reality more and more.

Tom was used to running around with his friends on the reserve, playing games with his brother or chasing after the cows. At the Institute, every day was structured and everything had rules. He was not allowed to speak his Onondaga language or practice his Native culture, he had no free time, and basically, school for Tom was no fun.

The rules, regulations and praying were too much for the young Tom, and a few weeks into his second year he ran away from the Institute. But he made the mistake of running home to his mother's house, and government officials found him and returned him to the school. However, the school could not hold onto him for long. A few weeks later he took off again, but this time he hid at his uncle's house, and soon the school gave up on him as just another lost Indian.

Years later, as an old man, Tom always told his family members that despite the relative poverty of the reserve, his time spent at the Mohawk Institute were the worst years of his life.

When he was sure the school was not looking for him anymore, Tom returned home to help his mother with the farming duties. Tom and his brother were now the men of the house, and Tom spent most of his time eking out what little sustenance the soil around their house could provide. He also wandered to the local farms where he got some seasonal work picking apples, gathering corn, tending to animals, or when he was lucky, got an odd job in the canning factories, stuffing into cans the same apples and corn he had picked earlier.

For the next several years he travelled from farm to farm working and sleeping wherever he could. It was during his down time that Tom fully embraced his childhood passion for running. After a hard week's labour in the field, Tom found solace in running for long periods. It was only him against the wind. He didn't have a boss telling him to work faster or to improve his quotas. Running was an escape for Tom, and he needed a place just for himself. And with each passing year he found he could run faster and farther.

It was while he was travelling between towns for work that he came across his first competitive race. Races were usually held during a town's local fair or festival at the end of harvest time, and since Tom was always around, he watched with great excitement as the best athletes from the town competed for a variety of trophies and prizes.

One of the most experienced runners at many of these races was the famous Mohawk runner Bill Davis. In 1901, Davis had earned an international reputation when he competed in the Boston Marathon and came in second place. Tom was instantly in awe of Davis, and the two became fast friends. Davis took Longboat under his wing and soon gave the young runner enough confidence to take the leap and enter his first competition.

In the first few races, Tom did not do all that well. He never had a dedicated training regimen, but he learned quickly that winning a five-mile run meant more than simply running the fastest. Winning a long-distance race took stamina, strength, courage and intelligence. When he ran for pleasure he was basically running against himself, but in a competition, other individuals were all vying for the same prize.

In the spring of 1905, barely 18 years old, Tom entered into his first big race at the annual Victoria Day five-mile race in Caledonia. The field of runners was tough, but Tom felt he could put in a serious challenge given all his training as well as the advice of Bill Davis to help him along.

It was the middle of the afternoon, and several thousand people milled about the Caledonia fair grounds in their Sunday best, catching up with old friends while children ran about chasing each other. All the day's activities suddenly came to a halt when it was announced the race would begin. Mothers plucked their children from their giggling packs while the men scurried off to the betting booth to wager on their favourite runners.

Tom took up his position at the starting line, and with the sound of the gun, bolted off the line. He ran so fast that by the midway point of the race, he could not even see one runner behind him. The men who had placed their bets earlier on other runners were now frantic as they watched this unknown Indian cruising to victory. But near the end of the race, Tom began to slow down. The blistering pace that he started with took a toll on his lungs, and the burning in his legs became harder and harder to ignore.

With just under a mile left in the race, he looked over his shoulder and saw another runner slowly gaining ground. Tom tried to push his body a little bit further, but his muscles had reached their limit. One runner (whose name was not preserved on record) seized the opportunity and passed Tom to capture first place. For his part, Tom barely kept the other runners at bay and finished the race in a respectable second place.

Tom wasn't too upset that he had lost the race; after all, he won a small prize and had everyone talking about his performance, but most importantly, he learned that he could compete with some of the best runners in the area. With a little more hard work and proper training, he vowed to return to Caledonia and take home the top prize.

Over the next year, Tom started a systematic training regimen. He knew that in order not to repeat the exhaustion he felt at the end of the Victoria

Day race in Caledonia, he had to extend his training distances beyond the five-mile length of the race. Only then would he be sure not to overwork his muscles and lungs. He quickly became a fixture on the roads around the reserve, and when he needed to increase his distances, he ran to neighbouring towns. Few if any believed him when he said he could run to the nearest towns, so one day, in order to prove to everyone just how far he had come in his training, he pulled a stunt that the entire reserve talked about for at least a month.

When Tom heard one day that his older brother was taking the horse and buggy to Hamilton, 15–20 kilometres away, he decided to prove to everyone he was not lying about running those distances. Giving his brother a half hour head start, Tom laced his shoes and took off for Hamilton. As his brother pulled into town, one of the first things he saw was Tom leaning up against a post with a huge grin on his face.

A year later the Victoria Day race in Caledonia rolled around, and Tom once more enrolled in the five-mile race. This time a buzz surrounded the race. No longer was Tom the unknown Indian runner, and the betting this year was skewed more in his favour. Those who took the risk and wagered on him were well rewarded. From the start of the race Tom led all runners and finished so far in front that people at the fair laughed at the other competitors. The name of Tom Longboat began to spread, and the public wanted more from the 18-year-old runner.

After the decisive win at the Caledonia race, Tom's mentor and friend Bill Davis knew that the young runner was ready for a higher level of competition. Urged on by Davis and the promise of a higher prize, Tom enrolled in the 1906 *Hamilton Herald* Around the Bay Race. But this was not your average local Canadian race. Past winners of the event included the first Canadian winner of the Boston Marathon, John Caffery, and William Sherring, who a few months later won the gold medal in the marathon at the 1906 Olympics in Athens, Greece.

But the Hamilton race was made to separate the men from the boys. At 30.5 kilometres, it was the longest race Tom had competed in to date, and he was challenged by some of the toughest competitors in the region. Some had travelled from the United States and even Great Britain to attend the prestigious race. The favourite in fact was the Englishman John Marsh who had set several records in England before emigrating to Canada. The oddsmakers did not look favourably on the teenage Indian runner, placing his odds at 100 to 1, and you can hardly blame them when they saw Tom show up at the starting line wearing a loose sweatshirt, a tattered bathing suit and cheap canvas shoes. Tom thought he had made it onto the racing circuit when he won the Caledonia race by such a huge margin, but in Hamilton, Tom was still an unknown.

The odds did not matter to Tom, though; he performed best under pressure, and he was exactly in the position he wanted. No one gave him a second look, not the oddsmakers, the runners, the coaches or the reporters, and Tom knew he had an advantage over the race course. No one paid him attention, and if he made any sort of challenge, they would not take it seriously.

Tom arrived at the starting line and stared straight ahead, focused intently on his goal of winning the race. The other runners took curious glances at the shabbily dressed Indian and scoffed at the poor fellow's attempt to look professional. Tom ignored them, however, and at the sound of the gun he set out in a sprint. At first, those who hadn't placed their bets on Tom were quite thankful after watching him break off the starting line, for Tom had a rather unorthodox style of running.

The style of running at the time was to take high, long strides with the arms tucked firmly to the body and up near the chest. Tom, however, preferred to keep his strides low to the ground with his feet barely lifting off the surface, and he kept his hands low and at hip level. It looked quite strange, but in actuality the style saved a lot of energy and enabled him to go farther than any other runner.

In this race, Tom did not burn through all his energy in the opening moments of the race but tucked himself neatly behind a group of runners not too far out from the leader. Timing his steps carefully, Tom was in a great position by the midway point of the race as the weaker runners began to fall off and only the stronger ones were left. By the time he reached the 25-kilometre mark, Tom had put all competitors behind him except for one.

John Marsh, the English running champion, had built up a nice lead early in the race, but his fast pace began to take its toll by the halfway point, and Tom seized the opportunity.

Over the next few kilometres, the two runners played an entertaining game of cat and mouse as one took the lead only to relinquish it a few minutes later. Marsh had played this sort of game before with young runners, and he knew from experience that their energy would wear off, and he could coast to victory. But to Marsh's surprise, even though Tom sped up and then fell back, he never lost any ground. The crowd still expected the young Indian to falter and the experience of Marsh to prevail, but suspense was beginning to build among the spectators.

Opinions began shifting with just a handful of kilometres left in the race. It was at this point that Marsh and Tom reached a steep hill along Hamilton's Burlington Beach. As anyone who has ever run uphill knows, it takes a far greater amount of energy to push your body uphill, and in a race, runners will often slow down considerably in order to save what little reserves they have left for the final sprint to the finish line. After almost two hours of running, the outcome of the race came down to this one moment.

The crowd gathered at the end of the course began cheering at the top of their lungs as the two competitors made their final push to the end. Tom knew that this was his moment, and he pushed his way up the hill, full steam ahead. Marsh's experience told him to save his energy for the final sprint, and he slowed down his pace for the uphill climb. It was the wrong move. The crowd could hardly believe their eyes as the great John Marsh let up his pace, allowing the Indian to surge ahead. Marsh had counted on Tom burning through his energy supply, but the teenager seemed to have a limitless amount to give. In the distance remaining, Marsh watched the lead he had carefully carved out for the past 30 kilometres slip away step by step as Tom peeled away in front of him.

Things almost turned into a disaster for Tom when he took a wrong turn with only a kilometre or two to the finish line. Luckily, some spectators got the tired teen back on track, and Tom was able to cross the line a full three minutes ahead of Marsh (in a time of 1:49:25 seconds off a course record), despite taking a wrong turn.

Some fans were absolutely jubilant at having seen such an amazing performance put on by a young inexperienced runner while others were extremely upset at the turn of events because they had placed their bets on the "sure" victory by the "experienced" runner.

The Indian boy in the tattered shoes and with the odd running style had defied all odds and won the prestigious Hamilton Around the Bay Race.

The day after the race, all the local papers ran the story of Tom Longboat's amazing victory. The Aboriginal teenager had captured the imagination of running fans everywhere, and it wasn't long before race promoters came calling with offers.

Tom was considered a novelty, and promoters wanted to use that to draw more people to their events. If people came out to see him just because he was Aboriginal, then he was fine by that, but first and foremost he wanted to be seen as a serious runner. But to achieve the status of runners such as William Sherring and John Caffery, Tom would need some help.

Chapter Two

Into the Ring

THERE WAS NO DOUBT in anyone's mind after Tom's performance at the Hamilton Around the Bay Race that the kid had talent and could potentially be one of the best runners in the world, but he was only 18 years old and was still wet behind the ears. Out in the wide world of sports, promoters and businessmen, Tom surely would have been eaten alive by the circling sharks without some help. He already had the raw talent to make it to the top, and he needed someone who could point him in the right direction when warranted. That right person happened to be at the Around the Bay Race, and he immediately recognized Tom's potential.

Harry Rosenthal was a bookbinder who worked out of the W.J. Gage & Co. publishing house in Toronto, and he was one of the biggest running fans in the region. He attended all the races he could when he wasn't working, and thereby became a self-professed expert in the sport. When he saw Longboat beat John Marsh in the Around the Bay Race, he knew he had witnessed a special talent. That was when he decided to offer Tom his services as his manager.

Rosenthal had never managed an athlete before, but he could not allow Tom's talent to go to waste. Rosenthal also recognized that Tom could make him some money on the professional running circuit. He figured that with his knowledge of the running circuit and Tom's natural charisma and talent, they could rake up a small fortune together. He immediately approached Tom with his proposal. At first Tom was hesitant to work with someone he didn't know, but Rosenthal's enthusiasm won him over and the two partnered up. It was the perfect arrangement for Tom. Rosenthal entered him in races, negotiated the expense money, booked transportation, took care of his living needs and simply handled all the small details so that Tom could focus on racing.

It was a pretty sweet deal for Rosenthal because he would be affiliated with a world-class athlete, profiting from placing lucrative bets on his runner and personally taking home a large portion of Tom's winnings. The arrangement wasn't the best deal for

Tom, but it was his only opportunity to advance his career in the running world and possibly make a living.

The first item of business to take care of was Tom's living situation. Rosenthal could not sell Tom to sports promoters if Tom remained on his reserve. He needed to leave the Six Nations Reserve and move to a city that had the market and audience for a person with Tom's skill, and that place was Toronto.

Toronto was unlike any other city Tom had ever seen. He had been through Hamilton, but Toronto had over 200,000 residents, streetcars at every turn and main streets wider and longer than anything he could have imagined. He had come from the reserve that boasted several thousand residents. Toronto at the turn of the 20th century was a major industrial town with a developing financial centre at its core. There was the University of Toronto, the art galleries, the hospitals, the wealthy homes, all things Tom had never seen on the reserve. Life back home was calm, peaceful and relaxed, and Tom found his first exposure to the emerging modern world to be difficult at first.

To help ease him into Toronto life, Rosenthal set up Tom with a room in the house he shared with his widowed mother. It wasn't a palace by any means, but it was warm and comfortable.

In between races, though, Tom needed to work, and Rosenthal helped him in that capacity as well, getting him a job with his publishing company working as a general office clerk. The work was tough for someone used to being outdoors most of the day, but Tom had a goal and wasn't about to let an office job deter him from that.

He didn't have to stay in the office for long, because just two weeks after his arrival in Toronto, Rosenthal signed him up for his next race.

The 1906 Ward Marathon (falsely named because it was only a 15-mile race [24 kilometres] where a true marathon is 26 miles, 385 yards in length [approx. 42 kilometres]) was an annual event that attracted some of the city's best runners. The race started at the base of Toronto's High Park, looped around Lakeshore Road, then along a dirt road back to the park.

Rosenthal knew his protégé had the talent to win the race, but a few runners made him a little nervous that his betting might go sour. Toronto's West End YMCA had been producing highly competitive runners for some time, and they had the best chance that year of winning the race. Tom's toughest challenger was a young runner from the YMCA named Bill Cumming. This brash youngster had a similar reputation among running fans as a highly energetic finisher, but his Achilles' heel was that the boy had never run anything close to a 15-mile race. If Cumming was going to win, he would need to have the race of his life. Unfortunately, he had a race that almost cost him his life.

Oddsmakers for the Ward Marathon were placing their bets based on recent performances, and for the first time, Tom was at the top of their list. Cummings was in close competition and wanted to prove to his home crowd that he had staying power on the racetrack. Seventy-three competitors left the starting line at the sound of the gun, but by the halfway mark it appeared that the race was between Cumming and Tom. But a keener observer would have noticed that despite Cumming's pace, he was breathing heavily and beginning to run erratically.

The first signs of fatigue had set in. Despite the pressures of the race, Cumming was not about to quit. He pushed his body to the edge to gain a few steps on Tom. The strategy excited the fans but took its toll on Cumming. Just over the halfway mark of the race, Cumming began to stumble and then passed out from exhaustion. With no other runner left capable of challenging Tom for the win, he cruised across the finish line with not another runner in sight. Tom had triumphed in the big city.

Tom went back to working at the office and trained in his spare time once fall settled in. He was not really expecting to race until spring, but Rosenthal was nothing if not persistent and entered Tom in a race on Christmas Day! Rosenthal was definitely proving to be driven, but Tom never minded the chance to get out in the fresh air.

The Christmas Day race took place in Hamilton, and luckily for the runners, the temperature was rather mild with no snow on the ground, but the race course was pot marked by hundreds of icy patches. Despite the pitfalls, Tom presented himself at the starting line ready for action. He had heard before the race that the young Bill Cumming had entered as well and was probably looking for revenge after the humiliating loss at the Ward Marathon. Cumming knew he had a better chance in this race since it was a 10-mile run (16 kilometres) and the stamina of Longboat would not matter much.

The race would simply come down to who wanted it more, and by the halfway point of the race it appeared to be the case. Tom and Cumming were running side by side, leaving all other challengers behind. If the race continued in that manner, it would certainly mean a sprint to the finish for one of the runners. Everything was going smoothly for the leaders when a group of spectators who had placed their bets on another runner deliberately sent a cart crashing into Longboat and Cumming. The two runners were sent tumbling to the cold ground, but with the adrenaline from the assault still running through their veins, both men were able to bounce back and continue the race as if nothing had occurred.

The two runners stayed at each other's side for the remainder of the race, making for a dramatic sprint to the finish. Cumming had a history of strong finishes, but the day once again belonged to Tom. Reaching deep within his energy reserves, he picked up the pace in the last few hundred metres of the race. Cumming tried to match Tom's speed but just couldn't catch up. In all his races to date, he had never really been challenged up until the final stretch, and although Cumming managed to find an extra gear to push for the end, Tom was able to answer each step and win the race. Not only did he win the race but he also broke the previous record by two minutes.

Tom liked winning, but Rosenthal liked it even more. The once lowly bookbinder was now the manager of one of the area's most successful athletes, and he was relishing every moment. Money was coming in, and with the attention of the press, Rosenthal did not want to stop the momentum. His desire to keep winning at all costs led to Rosenthal's first bad decision as a manager.

Wanting to keep the victories coming, after the Christmas Day marathon victory, Rosenthal entered

Tom in an indoor race on February 11, 1907, in Buffalo, New York. But the odds were stacked against Tom before he even stepped out onto the track.

The race was a simple one-on-one competition against one of the best indoor track runners at the time, American George Bonhag. In addition to racing one of the top runners in North America, the distance of the race was another factor Tom had to contend with. At three miles (4.8 kilometres), the race was the shortest distance Tom had ever run in competition. Throughout his brief running career Tom had always been a middle to long distance specialist, seemingly thriving off the challenge of pushing his body to its limits. The race would be a difficult one.

When Rosenthal and Tom made the journey to Buffalo for race day, Tom walked into the stadium where the race would be held and was shocked to see just over 8000 fans. Some were holding signs in support of Bonhag while others had less than polite slogans denouncing Tom. They made it more than obvious that he was on Bonhag's turf.

Topping disadvantage upon disadvantage, Tom's manager omitted to tell him that special shoes were necessary when running on an artificial surface. The shoes Tom wore were the same ones he had used for all his earlier races—simple rubber-soled athletic shoes that lacked sufficient grip to keep him from sliding over the indoor wooden track surface.

At the sound of the starter's pistol, both men broke out into a steady run, but Bonhag took an early lead because Tom had yet to acclimate to the track's running surface. But despite having to run on the unfamiliar surface, through the first half of the race Tom managed to stay within a competitive distance. It was clear that experience was going to win this race when Bonhag took and held the inside position of the track, which forced Tom to run along the outside and therefore cover more track. Bonhag in effect was running a shorter distance with each lap. Tom's rubber-soled shoes did not help him on the corners as he had to slow down each time in order not to slip on the track.

Throughout the entire race, Bonhag seemed to have his whole strategy mapped out. In the corners, instead of taking advantage of Tom's slower speed to move ahead, Bonhag purposely slowed down to take a rest of sorts in order to retain some energy for the final push to the finish.

Despite all these strikes against him, Tom still managed to make the race competitive, keeping up with Bonhag through to the last lap. Upon seeing the finish line up ahead, both men reached deep within themselves to find whatever remaining bit of energy they had and sprinted to the finish.

The fans in attendance watched with suspense as the runners remained shoulder to shoulder through the last few steps to the end. But it was Bonhag who had more to give in the race, and he beat Tom by a single stride. The crowd erupted in applause (well, the ones who bet on Bonhag did anyway), rising to their feet to salute the effort given by the two men, while both Tom and Bonhag staggered around the track trying to catch their breath.

Sure, Tom had lost, Rosenthal cried out loud in all the papers the next day, but despite all the odds stacked against Tom—the slippery rubber shoes, running against an experienced indoor racer, getting the inside track most of the race, and competing in front of a hostile crowd—he had put in the race of his life. Tom for his part simply put the experience behind him and returned to his job at the publishing house and continued to focus on his training for the next race.

Chapter Three

Beantown Beatdown

So, when Persia was dust, all cried, "To Acropolis!

Run, Pheidippides, one race more! the meed is thy due!

Athens is saved, thank Pan, go shout!" He flung down his shield

Ran like fire once more: and the space 'twixt the fennel-field

And Athens was stubble again, a field which a fire runs through,

Till in he broke: "Rejoice, we conquer!" Like wine through clay,

Joy in his blood bursting his heart, – the bliss!

– Robert Browning

THE MARATHON is one of the most ancient tests of athleticism, endurance, courage and mental toughness in the world. Simply put, it is one person against 42.195 kilometres of track. Battling heat, cold, wind exhaustion and mental fatigue, the marathon runner's greatest obstacle is himself. Many have attempted to complete this most arduous of tasks, and only few have triumphed.

The history of the marathon can be traced to ancient Greece in 490 BC in the village of Marathon at the feet of a messenger named Pheidippides. The story goes that the mighty Persian army, which had conquered much of the Middle East, Egypt and Turkey, had set its sights on attaining the prize jewel of the Mediterranean, Greece. Emperor Darius I and his armies had been slowly moving west, absorbing the various city states and kingdoms along the way. On his path of empire building, Darius I conquered the Greek cities along the shores of what is now modern Turkey, and as a result, several of the Greek city states (namely Athens) supported a revolt against their new Persian overlord in what became known as the Ionian Revolt. From 499 BC to 493 BC, the Persians and Greek cities fought a battle for control of the land. Although the Greek cities were eventually crushed, Darius I was furious that Athens and the other Greek cities had supported the revolt. And with the revolt out of the way, Darius I focused his attention on Athens and the rest of the Greek cities for having meddled in the rebellion.

Darius I and his army pushed their way through Asia Minor, conquering the Macedonians and the Thracians on their journey into Northern Greece. By 490 BC, the army had reached the Greek city of Marathon, and a bloody battle began on the plains surrounding the city. For five days the two armies fought, until the Greek soldiers finally made a final push and slaughtered the remaining Persian soldiers. The battle was won, but to ensure that no further soldiers were being diverted from the other frontlines, a messenger had to be sent to Athens to deliver the news of victory. That messenger, according to legend, was a man named Pheidippides.

With the message in hand, Pheidippides was dispatched from Marathon to deliver the information to the Athenian generals some 42 kilometres away. With Hermes, ancient Greek messenger to the gods, at his side, Pheidippides ran as quickly as possible without pausing for rest or water. Upon reaching the town centre, he cried out "Rejoice! We conquer!" and then died on the spot.

While the story of Pheidippides is most likely just that, a story, it perfectly illustrates the gruelling challenge that any runner must face when doing a marathon. During the Olympic Games of Ancient Greece, the marathon was one of the major events where competitors often ran half or even fully naked. The games were a celebration of the human form and all its possibilities, and nothing was more purely human than the naked form.

But times changed, and runners put their clothes back on when the modern Olympics returned in 1896. The marathon was the premiere running event of those Olympics, and 25 runners competed to be the winner of the first modern Olympic marathon. Among those runners was one American named Arthur Blake. Olympic glory was not in Blake's destiny, however, because at the half way point of the race, he collapsed and never completed the marathon. Now Arthur Blake might have remained just a footnote in Olympic history had it not been for one fact: when he returned from Greece to his hometown of Boston, he, with the help of the Boston Athletic Association, helped organize the first Boston Marathon, held in 1897.

Various marathon events in North America operated at the same time as the Boston race, but no other event garnered the same attention and mystique. Winners of those early Boston Marathons later went on to succeed in the Olympics and on the professional racing circuit. For Tom Longboat, racing in the Boston Marathon was his destiny.

The moment that Harry Rosenthal had first laid eyes on Tom Longboat at the Hamilton Around the

Bay Race, he knew he was meant for one race. The training and competitions that Tom had done were all working towards that spring day of April 19, 1907. It was the perfect timing. Tom was at the peak of his running career, and everyone seemed to know his name. If he could win this race, Rosenthal envisioned, the next stop would be the world stage. Tom's manager was nothing if not ambitious, but it was exactly those ambitions that got Rosenthal into some trouble with the Amateur Athletic Union (AAU), an association responsible for keeping order in and professionalism out of amateur sports in the United States.

After the success of the Bonhag race and the general public's growing interest in Tom Longboat, Rosenthal and the New York Athletic Club (NYAC) discussed the possibility of a rematch. Rosenthal believed in his client's ability to win the match, but he told the NYAC he needed $150 in expense money in order to enter Tom in the race. When the AAU and the Canadian Amateur Athletic Union (CAAU) got wind of the amount he had requested, they immediately took Rosenthal for a crook and suspended him and Tom from any further racing in the United States.

This was not a good turn of events for Tom as it directly threatened the future of his running career. In order to rectify the situation, both the U.S. and

Canadian amateur sports governing bodies informed Tom that he would have to fire Rosenthal as his manager if he wanted to be reinstated. Although Tom had become quite fond of his manager, living and working side by side as they did, he knew that he had to obey the wishes of the amateur associations or his career would be finished.

Needing guidance and a means of funding his running ventures, Tom joined up with Toronto's West End YMCA and began training with other runners, including former rival Bill Cumming. It was the perfect spot for Tom. The facilities were top quality, experienced coaching staff were already in place, and the Y provided Tom with the support he needed to enter future competitions. Tom was able to get all of these issues resolved in time for him to pack his bags and depart for Boston in mid-April for his first Boston Marathon.

Little did Tom realize, though, caught up as he was in his little bubble of working for the publishing company and training at the YMCA, that his celebrity status had skyrocketed in recent months. His impressive list of wins had caught the public's attention, and even before stepping off the train in Boston, the media had been gearing up for his arrival.

Because he was Aboriginal, Tom held a certain mystique to the public, and especially the sportswriters who came up with all sorts of nicknames for him, from the obvious "Onondaga Wonder" to the alliterative "Caledonia Cyclone" to the slightly awkward and politically insensitive "Streak of Bronze." Desperate to capitalize on Tom's fame, one Boston newspaper, not having a photo of Tom, published the picture of a Native football player they had on file and simply claimed in the caption that it was Tom Longboat. It didn't seem to really matter at the time; everybody wanted a piece of Tom even if it meant a fake picture.

Due to the tenacity of the Boston media, Tom remained secluded from public view until the day of the race. Upon waking up on the morning of April 19, Tom felt an unseasonably cold breeze smack his face as the temperature dipped to a low of 4°C with clouds low enough to reach up and touch. These were not the ideal conditions to be running in, but Tom was from the north and had a certain tolerance to the cold that his lower state American competitors lacked. Despite his ability to handle the cold, Tom wore a sweater over his official runner's jersey to keep his muscles warm and ready for the race ahead.

Tom gathered at the starting line with the 126 other competitors, and all eyes in the crowd seemed to be aimed directly at him. Expectations of him were high, but Tom simply focused on running the same way he did in training. He knew that the only person who could make him win the race was himself.

The route of the track was now overflowing with spectators. Cheers rang out from the crowd as they called out the names of their favourite runners. The excitement in the air began to mount well before the sound of the starter pistol. When the referee raised his gun in the air, the crowd suddenly fell silent, then with a bang, the noise from the fans broke like a wave and propelled the runners forward.

Tom remained a good distance back from the lead runners as he did not want to expend all his energy right from the outset, and he also wanted to get his body accustomed to the cold. The YMCA trainer who had accompanied Tom on the trip followed him throughout the race and shouted for him to pick up the pace. After running for a few kilometres, Tom finally removed his sweater, tossed it to his trainer, and began to pick up the pace, but not before giving his trainer a big smile, as if to say, "Don't worry. I got this."

Little by little Tom began to catch up to the leaders, and after 40 minutes of running he held firmly onto the lead with two other runners. One of the runners was Sam Mellor, a veteran of running competitions out of New York City who had won the

Boston Marathon in 1902. The other runner was the 18-year-old upstart Charlie Petch out of Toronto who came out of nowhere and was the definite underdog of the three.

The crowds along the race course grew as the runners inched closer to the finish line. It was later estimated by the Boston police that some 200,000 people had lined up along the route to cheer on their favourite runners, but the majority of the people were trying to get as close to the finish as possible in hopes of seeing the winner race to victory.

So many people were on the course that at one point the path the runners were on began to narrow as people crowded in to get a better view. One such spectator got a little too close to the runners, and the bicycle he was riding caught Sam Mellor's legs and sent him falling to the ground. It was a hard fall, and Mellor did not recover in time to be a contender in the race. Tom and Charlie Petch seized the moment to take a commanding lead over their unlucky opponent. Mellor did manage to return to his feet and get back in the race, but he could never match the leaders' pace, ultimately falling out of contention. The race for the Boston Marathon was now down to two young runners who just three years earlier no one had ever even heard of.

Although Tom had a slight edge in experience over his younger opponent, Petch did not ease his pace for one moment, matching Tom stride for stride. As they passed the large crowds, groups of girls screamed out after Tom, and he waved, flashed a big grin, and continued on his merry way. While Tom was acting like he was out for a leisurely jog, Petch was running at full steam. Those who were aware of Tom's running style were waiting for him to make his move and end the game he seemed to be playing with his opponent. That time came when they reached the infamous Newton Hills portion of the race.

Consisting of two steep slopes, this part of the course would either make or break the two men. Petch decided the best plan of action was to approach the hill with caution and save his energy for the final sprint. That decision led to his demise in the race. While Petch hung back, Tom chose to pick up the pace and attack the two hills, so that by the time he crested the last hill, he had put a few hundred metres between him and Petch. The sight of Longboat pulling away seemed to take all the energy out of Petch, and he eventually finished the race in sixth place. Tom, meanwhile, was cruising towards the finish line with no other runners in sight.

The crowd had Tom all to themselves, and nearing the finish line, they pushed forward to get a glimpse of their new hero. They gathered so close to Tom that he had to deftly avoid some of the spectators who wanted to reach out to touch him. After the close call with the crowd, it was a straight on to the finish.

Tom finished the race in 2 hours, 24 minutes and 25 seconds, five minutes faster than the previous record held by fellow Canadian winner John Caffery. Under those same cloudy skies that welcomed the runners at the beginning of the race, Tom received the three-foot-high statue of the messenger god Mercury from the governor of Massachusetts. People crowded the stage wanting to hear a few words from their champion, and when asked by a reporter how he felt about the race, Tom replied with characteristic confidence, "I knew I could win the race and break the record." At that he left the crowds and returned to his hotel to rest and have a nice steak dinner.

It must have been an incredible sight to see as some 200,000 people cheered on a young Native man for winning the Marathon, a man who without the distinction of that three-foot statue probably wouldn't have been welcomed into their homes or been allowed to date their daughters. The irony of the situation most likely was not lost upon Tom.

Upon hearing word of Tom's win, Toronto began planning a big party in anticipation of their native son's return. City council set aside funds for a parade, a reception at city hall, a gold medal and a $500 fund to go towards giving Tom a proper education. (Tom never received that money, though. Because of a lengthy bureaucratic process, his heirs did not receive the money until 1980.)

As the train pulled into Toronto Union Station, Tom was greeted by thousands of fans and the loud blaring of several bands. The throng of people carried Tom up Bay Street to City Hall where Mayor Coatsworth was waiting to present Tom with the gifts from the city. After the mayor made his speech, the crowd quieted down as Tom was about to speak. He addressed his words to the mayor and the city of Toronto, "Mr. Mayor, I thank you kindly for the splendid reception, for the medal and the City grant and I shall try to prove myself worthy of the City's kindness."

With those few humble words, Tom left the stage while the bands struck up and the crowd continued in their revelry. At the reception dinner afterwards, while people drank wine and told him how important and great he was, Tom could not help but feel the pain of loneliness as all the people who really knew him were back on the reserve.

Chapter Four

Across the Pond

His trainers are to be congratulated, not only on having such a docile pupil, but on being able to show such excellent results from their regime. It is to be hoped that Longboat's success will not develop obstinacy on his part and that he will continue to be manageable. If he does not lose his head or begin to break faith with the public, he has other triumphs in store and as much adulation as any mortal man could wish.

– Toronto Star editorial after Tom Longboat's 1907 Boston Marathon win

AS EVIDENCED FROM the media writings about him, Tom Longboat was certainly treated with interest and fascination, but not necessarily with respect. The above passage is just one example of how Tom was viewed as a commodity that had to be watched, and that despite his success, underneath it all he was still branded for what he looked like and not what he accomplished. From the day he stepped into the white world at the Mohawk Institute in Brantford, Tom was well aware of the differences between the two cultures. Through it all he tried to remain true to himself and to keep his independent spirit. However, after the Boston Marathon, with his increased popularity and the growing attention paid to him, Tom once again felt his world closing in on him. He sensed that the people around him were trying to control his every move. And the main source of this oppression was coming from his new coach, Charles Ashley.

Ashley respected Tom's talent but had no respect for him as an individual. He seemed to treat Tom like the Toronto Star's description of him: "a docile pupil" in need of training. Ashley had a strict set of rules for his runners that often reminded Tom of his days at the Mohawk Institute. Tom's new coach insisted that his runners have no alcohol, no involvement with women, and he set up a training schedule that did not allow for much free time.

Tom was dedicated to his sport, but he was, after all, still a young man who liked to go out on the town, flirt with pretty girls and have the occasional drink or two. What was the point of putting in all that hard work if you could not enjoy the fruit of your labour? The constant preaching and lectures on self-discipline reminded Tom too much of the "education" he had received as a youth at the Mohawk Institute, and in June 1907 Tom left the West End YMCA and quickly found a home with the Irish Canadian Athletic Club (ICAC).

The ICAC was the perfect venue for Tom. The organization was less structured than the YMCA, with some members who, like Tom, were enrolled in the hopes of making it to the professional ranks, while others simply joined for the exercise and fun of competition the Y offered. This led to a laid-back atmosphere among the athletes and proved to be the ideal place for Tom at the time. And it was at the ICAC that Tom met his new trainer and eventual manager Tom Flanagan.

An avid sportsman, Tom Flanagan was a fixture of the Toronto social scene. Part owner of the Grand Central Hotel, he was widely known for his indulgences and his adoration of sports. This adoration and the money to back it up enabled him to take on the managerial role to several athletes he considered talented enough. One such athlete was the famous heavyweight boxing champion of the world, Jack Johnson. Flanagan had started up the ICAC in order to be closer to young talent in the early stages of their careers. In June 1907, he set his eyes on Tom

Longboat and saw a prosperous future ahead for both of them.

From the moment Tom joined the club they set about promoting their famous new member by putting his face on posters and signing him up to a variety of races. One of the most infamous was a meeting that July at the Ottawa Carnival before 8000 fans.

Infamous, because Tom would be racing across five miles of track against a team of three runners, all from his home ICAC, and all of whom were experienced in the long-distance race. Adding to the infamy was the fact that one of the runners, James Marsh (no relation to John Marsh), was also a part-time sportswriter who in his earlier columns had been less than polite in his treatment of Tom, writing racist rants such as, "In my time, I've interviewed everything from a circus lion to an Eskimo chief, but when it comes to being the original dummy, Tom Longboat it is. Interviewing a Chinese Joss or a mooley cow is pie compared to the task of digging anything out of Heap Big Chief T. Longboat." And after the race in Ottawa, Marsh's disdain for Tom only grew further.

The race began without any major incident or surprises. The first two runners did what they could to keep Tom from pulling too far ahead, so by the time Marsh entered the race, both men were shoulder to shoulder. Marsh did pull ahead at one point, but Longboat kicked in that extra gear he always seemed to have and caught up with Marsh by the final stretch.

The two men had all in attendance on their feet cheering as they sprinted to the tape. With just a few feet to go, Marsh led the race by a few inches, but in the last two steps, Tom again somehow managed to find that little extra bit of energy and lunged across the line to win the race, breaking the Canadian five-mile speed record in the process.

Tom not only won the race, but he also defeated three of Toronto's best distance runners, and for good measure had embarrassed the pompous Marsh. It probably did not help Marsh's articles that a month later Tom went on to defeat Marsh again, this time against five runners over a four-mile course at the Toronto Police Games on August 22, 1907. For the remainder of his running career, Tom always had to deal with Marsh's overly critical and borderline racist comments in his articles.

Over the next several months, with the help of his manager, Tom ran a series of races across eastern Canada. He took on his old rival from the Around the Bay Race, John Marsh, in a five-mile race and beat him again; he returned and repeated as champion of the 1907 Ward Marathon; and he embarrassed Irish American runner J.J. Daley so much in a five-mile race that Daley quit halfway through.

These were boom times for Tom, and especially for his manager. Flanagan was proving to be a much better manager than Rosenthal, and at each event Tom participated in, Flanagan made sure he pulled in a significant adoring and paying crowd. For Flanagan, Tom Longboat was turning out to be a cash cow. Because he was classified as an amateur runner, Tom was not allowed to take money for any of the races he won, so he was entirely dependent on Flanagan to provide him with a place to live, the food in his stomach and the small allowance for an occasional night on the town.

But in addition to the prize money he was collecting on a regular basis, Flanagan made most of his money in the betting parlours. Those foolish enough to bet against Tom gave large sums of cash to the Flanagan cause. His betting got so brazen that he even wagered a friend that Tom could outrun his friend's horse from Hagersville to Caledonia, a distance of about 18 miles (29 kilometres). The horse managed to take the lead off the start but was nowhere to be seen when Tom crossed the finish line in Caledonia.

However, all the money surrounding Tom was not good for his image. He was after all still an amateur, and just like what had occurred earlier

Bibliothèque Saint-Claude Library

with Tom's previous manager, Henry Rosenthal, if the amateur associations got wind of any funny business with money, they would strip him of his amateur status. To retain that rank, Flanagan put on a public relations campaign to show that Tom was doing his part in the community. Flanagan gave him an easy job working in a cigar store that he renamed Tom Longboat Cigars. Tom simply stood behind the counter and greeted customers, giving the appearance that he was earning his own money.

Both Tom and Flanagan had every intention of going professional, but there was one competition that Tom wanted to get out of the way before heading down that road.

Going professional certainly would have its benefits. In the dawn of the 20th century, races between the top professionals drew crowds by the thousands in arenas around North America and Europe; thousands of fans were willing to pay top dollar to get a glimpse of their favourites and bet on them in the process. The purses were of course larger in comparison to the amateur races, and the money Tom took home was a matter of public record; going professional also meant that his financial gains from running would not be available for everyone to see.

Yet despite all of Flanagan's attempts to appease the amateur associations, the American Amateur Union did not like what they saw happening in Tom's career. It was impossible to miss the extravagance that followed Tom as he rolled into each new town for a race. The bands, the comfortable carriages and silk top hats were seen as the calling cards of a pro, and the AAU banned Tom from any future races under its jurisdiction.

This turn of events was devastating news to Tom because it meant he could not defend his title in the Boston Marathon. Fortunately, the Canadian Amateur Athletic Union refused to follow along with the American ban. This allowed Tom to continue to race in Canada, but most importantly it allowed him the chance to make the Canadian Olympic team for the 1908 Summer Games in London, England. The CAAU officials had every reason to ban Tom, but with the eyes of the world on the Olympics, they decided to give the nation's best runner a shot at bringing home Olympic glory.

When the Olympics returned from the pages of history in 1896, the world had not yet fully embraced the spirit of friendly global competition. The initial Olympics were ill attended and underrepresented by the nations of the world. But as the years passed, countries caught on to the spirit, and athletes viewed the competition as the ultimate proving ground of their talent on the world stage. Canada really first began to take notice of the Olympics only after the 1904 Games in St. Louis in which most of the 41 Canadian participants returned home with medals. The high medal count was because many of the top athletes from European countries hadn't wanted to make the long Atlantic journey to the United States. But interest increased ten-fold in Canada when William Sherring won the 1906 Olympic gold in the marathon before a decidedly pro-Greek crowd in Athens. No one had expected the diminutive Canadian runner to factor in the race, and Sherring's underdog story captivated Canadian racing fans. With the arrival of Tom Longboat onto the racing scene, Canada was once again expected to take home the gold for the Olympic's premiere event.

Up until 1908, the marathon did not have an official recognized distance. The Ward Marathon was set at 15 miles (24.1 kilometres), the first Olympics in 1896 was 24 miles (38.6 kilometres), and the Boston Marathon was 25 miles (40.2 kilometres). In 1908 an established distance for the marathon was still not in place, so Olympic officials set the race to start at the town centre of Windsor and to finish at the Shepard's Bush Stadium in London, which was a distance of just under 26 miles (41.8 kilometres).

But the long-distance race had long been a passion for the royal family, and they requested that the starting point be extended to the royal grounds of Windsor Castle. The new running distance was now 26 miles, 385 yards (approximately 42 kilometres), and this became the standard distance for future marathons.

The Canadian Olympic trials were scheduled for a few months before the games, and the pressure was on for all the athletes to perform their best, because it would be the first year the Canadian government would sponsor their efforts. In previous years, athletes had to finance their own way to the games.

As well as the luxury of having government money to ease the cost of the trip to London, the track athletes also had the added benefit of former Olympic gold winner William Sherring as their head coach.

Being able to attend the Olympic trials was really important to Longboat, but he was forced to miss the event because he had a bad outbreak of boils. It was an unlucky break, but Tom's reputation as a stellar runner was enough to get him added to the team without doing the trials. In reality, riots would have broken out had Tom not been allowed to join the team travelling to the Olympics.

In June, Flanagan took his star athlete to his old family plot in Limerick, Ireland, to get an early start on his training. But it was not the peaceful retreat that Tom had hoped for. Word of his arrival spread throughout the town and surrounding villages, and on many of his training runs throughout the countryside, police were often needed to keep the hundreds and sometimes thousands of spectators who came out to see the Native runner.

The international press also loved to watch Tom train, and they wrote daily articles on his progress, but all the attention he received wasn't the best atmosphere for Tom to be in. So a week before the start of the games, Flanagan moved Tom to London and restricted the public's access to the athlete. Tom spent his time there resting and planning his strategy for the Olympics.

In the meantime, word reached the Canadian track team that famed marathon runner John Caffery had taken the opportunity to run the race course, and he did not have pleasant things to say about its condition. First, the condition of the track was not conducive to running a marathon. The path was as hard as nails, which meant that a runner's shoes had to absorb a lot of shock and would take a lot of wear during the race.

The runners also had to contend with a route that sent them through a variety of twists and turns that led to some passages so narrow that only one runner at a time could squeeze through. The marathon wasn't going to be easy, but Tom had come through under more difficult conditions during his running career, so not much could stop him from challenging for the gold.

On the day of the race, July 24, 1908, 58 runners gathered on the front lawn of Windsor Castle before the members of the Royal family. The weather was not exactly a typical English summer day; rain the previous day had combined with an extreme summer heat wave and made the air thick, humid and hard to breathe.

Just after 2:00 PM, British Lord Desborough fired the starter's pistol and the runners set out. The pace of the runners at the beginning was subdued, in part for respect to the royal crowd in attendance and the extreme midday heat.

But once out of the royal courtyard and into the screaming crowd, the runners picked up their pace. After the halfway mark, the leaders in the race were down to a few runners.

The pace was still going ahead feverishly as the top runners tried to put some distance between themselves and Tom. The strategy had never worked for the competitors in any of Tom's past races as he always had extra energy in the final leg of the race to make up any distance.

However, anyone cheering for Tom that day would have noticed that the Canadian runner did not look good in the final stretch of the marathon. His pace had become laboured as was his breathing under the intense glare of the sun and the oppressive humidity. Into the 20-mile mark of the race, Tom was just holding onto second position when he entered a clearing that was open to the heat and the blaring sun. Suddenly, he began to stumble, and he fell to the ground, shaking from heat exhaustion.

Immediately, people ran to his side while the other runners simply ran past the prostrate Canadian runner. An Olympic official walked over and declared Tom unfit to continue the race. Tom was carried into an awaiting car and driven to the finish line at Shepard's Bush Stadium. The winner of the race, Dorando Pietri, also had difficulty in the race. He fell down several times, suffering from extreme heat exhaustion, and race officials picked him off the track and basically pushed him to the finish.

Although he was originally awarded the victory, the second place runner, American John Hayes, complained that without the help of officials he might have passed the Italian runner. After some discussion among officials, it was later decided that Hayes and not Pietri be awarded the gold medal.

While the other runners celebrated, Flanagan and Tom tried to explain to the throng of reporters what had occurred to dash Tom's hopes of a gold medal. Flanagan spouted several excuses, from Tom's inadequate shoes to the winding, unfamiliar track, whereas Tom simply blamed the extreme heat and humidity for his inability to complete the race. But one Canadian official had a more sinister explanation for Tom's failure. In his official report at the end of the Olympics, J.H. Crocker wrote:

All say that Longboat was running well at the twentieth mile in second place. He collapsed without warning and complained of a severe pain in his head... As soon as he was brought in I went over and examined him carefully ... I found a weak pulse—the respiration was very slow—a pinpoint pupil which was not sleep. To all appearances, someone had got anxious and thinking to help the Indian by giving him a stimulant, had given him an overdose.

The stimulant in question was reported to be strychnine. Most commonly used today as an ingredient in rat poison, strychnine, taken in very small doses, was sometimes used in those days as an energizing agent for athletes. Taken in larger doses, it can cause the body to react in nearly the exact same way Tom had during his collapse on the Olympic track. A greater dose often results in death.

Tom never would have knowingly taken a drug to win the race, and it was more likely something that was given to him by his manager. Flanagan was the one person who had put a lot of time, energy and money into Tom's running career, and if Tom would have won the gold, it would have meant heavy monetary returns in the future.

Tom was incredibly disappointed by the dramatic turn of events at the Olympics, but he returned to North America with a new goal ahead of him.

Chapter Five

Welcome to the Jungle

AFTER THE MEDIA CRAZINESS of the Olympics, Tom took some time off from running to relax and get mentally prepared to train once again. Flanagan wanted to push Tom back into the running circuit almost immediately after arriving back on North American soil, but Tom wanted, almost needed, a break after all the attention and media circus that had surrounded his run in London.

When the Olympics were over, many in the sports world thought Tom's time in the spotlight of the running world had come to an end and that if he continued to enter races he faced a career that would end in shame. To avoid such a fate, Flanagan tried to get Tom back on a rigorous training regimen, but Tom preferred to take his time getting back into racing. He took long walks, played lacrosse and socialized with friends. It was an attitude that annoyed Flanagan to no end, but Tom was not going to alter the way he lived for his manager. He hadn't done it for the Mohawk Institute, he hadn't done it for Rosenthal, and he certainly wasn't going to start now.

After a few short weeks repose, Tom went back to doing what he loved most. His first race since coming back from the Olympics was on August 15, 1908, in a head-to-head three-mile run against Fred Simpson in Hamilton. Simpson, a Native from Peterborough, Ontario, was not simply some easy low-grade runner Flanagan had set Tom up to destroy. In fact, running against Simpson was a true test of Longboat's ability to bounce back from defeat, because Simpson had finished sixth in the same Olympic marathon that Tom didn't complete. A few thousand fans turned out to see the return of Tom Longboat; some to cheer him on and others to see if he would fail. But it turned out not to be a good day for the ill-wishers as Tom easily handled Simpson on this side of the pond, finishing comfortably in the lead.

Just a few days later, Tom was back at it again at the Toronto Police Games to take on Percy Sellen, a fellow member of the Irish Canadian Athletic Club. It was only a five-mile race, but throughout the event Tom felt sluggish and didn't appear to have his normal blistering, confident pace. Sellen for his part had a relative easy race, and to everyone's surprise, Tom lost to him.

The sportswriters who had all said after Tom's defeat in the Olympic Marathon that it was only a matter of time before he failed, cried out in the papers that the legend of Tom Longboat had finally come to pass. While everyone around him shouted disaster, Tom simply took it all in stride and blamed his sluggishness on the heavy meal he had eaten before the race. And when the two men faced off again in another five-mile run three days later, Tom won that race with the ease that people had come to expect.

Tom had victory after victory over the next few weeks as he travelled around eastern Canada knocking back all the challengers to his title of "the greatest amateur runner the country had ever seen." After Tom won his third straight Ward Marathon by a margin of eight minutes over his nearest competitor, Canadian Amateur Athletic Union president William Stark exclaimed that, "he has proven himself the greatest long-distance runner of the century."

The accolades suited Tom just fine, but he was beginning to tire of the humble life. He had travelled across oceans, competed against the best runners in the world, and yet he was still working in a tiny cigar shop, totally dependent on the pittance of a wage his manager handed out. After all, Tom had new responsibilities now that he planned to marry.

At the beginning of 1908 he had met and won over a young lady named Lauretta Maracle from the Mohawk Reserve near the Bay of Quinte. But if Tom was going to marry Lauretta and start a family, he knew he could no longer live off the wages of an amateur. By late fall of that year, Tom decided to race as a professional.

The moment word got out that Tom was turning professional, offers started pouring in from promoters to get him to appear at their events. The first one that peaked Flanagan's interest was from a New York City promoter named Pat Powers. Fully intending to capitalize on the controversy from the Olympic marathon, Powers managed to wrangle several of the runners from the Olympics and planned a series of races at the marathon distance in Madison Square Garden.

On December 15, 1908, Tom was scheduled to take on disqualified Olympic gold winner Dorando Pietri in a rematch—it was what everyone had wanted since the moment Tom fell out of the marathon back in London. The rematch would prove once and for all who was the best runner in the

Tom Longboat (left) dressed in a fashionable top hat and jacket, standing next to Tom Eck, a local promoter (date unknown).

world, and a packed Madison Square Garden turned out to see the outcome.

With New York's substantial Italian community in attendance, the crowd began to applaud when Pietri emerged from the dressing room wearing a fur-lined coat and waving to his supporters. He paused for one moment to soak in the adulation, and a rain of flowers fell on his head welcoming him to the stadium.

Once the crowd had settled down and Pietri had found his seat, Tom emerged from the dressing room area to a welcome considerably less enthusiastic than the one Pietri had received. Tom was not as lavishly dressed as his competitor, but without all the hype and expectations he seemed more prepared and focused to run the race than his opponent.

When the two men were called to the starting line, the crowd suddenly cheered with excitement. Pietri was the first off the line, and he held that position for a good part of the race. But because Pietri was a good deal shorter than Tom, his legs had to work that little bit extra to cross the same distance, and after a while he showed signs of slowing down. Pietri's trainers attempted to revive him by spraying him with water and feeding him cups of coffee, but Pietri could not keep up the feverish pace he had started with, and Tom began to close in.

With longer legs and a leaner physique, the hardship of running a marathon was a lot less of a strain on Tom's body, but by the 20th mile, Flanagan had to start feeding him shots of water and sips of champagne to fuel Tom's energy. Despite the efforts of both sides of the coaching staff, the runners eased back on their pace with five miles to go in the race, occasionally even slowing down to a walk.

But it was Tom who had more energy, and inch by inch he started to pull away from Pietri. Into the

25th mile, the Italian runner showed the same signs of fatigue that nearly forced him out of the race in the Olympics. He lost the coordination in his legs, his arms fell to his side, and it looked as if any moment he might collapse to the ground.

Seeing their hero begin to stumble, the crowd tried to bring Pietri back to life by cheering him on, and it seemed to work as he started to catch up once again. But while moving through one corner, he tripped over his own feet and crashed into one of the barriers on the side of the track. He looked like he had just received a knockout punch from a heavyweight boxer.

The Olympic marathon runner was finished. The crowd could hardly believe their eyes as trainers, coaches and doctors rushed to Pietri's side while Tom continued along the track. Tom did not look fully fit himself, but he once again found that energy reserve and finished the race. When he crossed the line, he felt as though he had put on an extra 100 pounds. His coach rushed to his side, and Tom was immediately hoisted on someone's shoulders and paraded around Madison Square Garden to polite cheers. Tom happily retired to his hotel room to rest and prepare for a night of celebrations on the town. The *Globe* newspaper proudly declared the next day, "Longboat Retrieves His Olympic Defeat."

Upon returning to Toronto, Tom and his fiancée began the preparations for their wedding. Lauretta was a petite woman, but her size belied the iron will she was said to possess. Devoted to her Anglican beliefs, she insisted on having a church wedding, which meant Tom had to be baptized into the Anglican faith. He did not really mind all that much as he did it more to please his new bride than some overwhelming need for salvation. The media, however, saw his marriage to Lauretta through different eyes.

Tom Longboat had already proven himself to be the greatest runner Canada had ever seen, but to a lot of people, his accomplishments never erased the fact that he was an "Indian." Many people believed at the time that an Aboriginal person could be shown the ways of the white man but could never fully be "tamed." Longboat spoke the language of the dominant culture and dressed the same as they did, but deep down he was rooted in his Native culture.

Tom's soon-to-be-wife Lauretta Maracle not only looked like the proverbial "girl next door," but she also had fully embraced the ways of the white society. Rather than their marriage being considered a union between two lovers, the media put a greater significance on Tom's wedding. The *Globe* wrote one particularly prejudiced article about the marriage:

Interesting a study as the world's champion long distance runner makes—as Indian first and before all—with, over those deep racial attributes, the light veneer of the white man's ways and habits, of far deeper interest is the girl he is about to wed. Here the Indian traits are all well covered... Few would imagine that she had been born and raised on an Indian reservation and was of Indian blood. In every way she is a winsome little girl who has, as she says, been educated away from many of the traditions of her race. She does not like to talk of feathers, war paint, or other Indian paraphernalia. She is ambitious for Tom and if anybody can make a reliable man and good citizen of that elusive being, Thomas Longboat, it will be his wife.

On December 28, 1908, Tom wed his sweetheart in the small St. John the Evangelist Church in Toronto's business district. But while the church ceremony was small and subdued with fewer than 100 people in attendance, Tom's best man Tom Flanagan knew how to party and rented out Toronto's most lavish hall, Massey Hall, for the reception.

Since none of Tom's family or friends from back home on the reserve could make it to the wedding, Flanagan invited the entire city of Toronto to join in the celebration. Just over 1000 people showed up to see a spectacle filled with bands, comedians, acrobats, and a host of other entertainers Flanagan had hired to celebrate their union. The party was a success, but the young couple had no time for a honeymoon as one week later Flanagan booked Tom in another race.

Apparently Tom had not embarrassed Dorando Pietri enough, and his pride at having lost to an Indian had to be repaired. Tom accepted the challenge like he did all the others. The race, set at 25 miles (40 kilometres), was held at the 74th Armory in Buffalo, New York. Close to 8000 people filed into the arena for the start of the race.

Once again Pietri bolted off the starting line at the sound of the pistol, breaking out into a steady pace much faster than he had in his earlier race with Tom. But Pietri had learned nothing from that race. As had happened in the first race, Pietri's strategy appeared to work, because in the first few miles Tom struggled to keep up. Pietri nearly won the race by default when, in his haste to keep up, Tom slipped on the track and fell onto one knee opening up a large cut that sent a gush of blood down his leg. A hushed crowd watched as Tom slowly struggled to his feet in obvious pain. A loud chorus of cheers from the crowd quickly broke the silence as Tom not only re-entered the race but also managed to gain the ground he had lost on Pietri.

By the 20th mile, the Italian was once again showing the same signs of fatigue that had knocked him out of the race only a few weeks earlier. It was apparent to those in attendance that Tom's blistering pace and the sight of him coming at him simply sucked all the remaining energy from Pietri's legs. He knew his body had nothing left to give, and in that 20th mile he withdrew from the race, leaving Tom to finish out the race in front of a packed arena.

Without the pressure of a runner at his heels, Tom slowed his pace down, but with five more miles to cover, his cut knee started to swell. His feet pounded the track, his chest heaved from lack of oxygen, and his legs barely kept him up, but he still managed to stay on his feet; he walked across the finish line once again the victor. Despite his blistered feet, bleeding and swollen knee, and tired legs, Tom was on top of the world. He once again proved to be the best when put against the world's best. At just 21 years of age, he seemed poised for even greater achievements, but like all good stories, our hero had to first face adversity before reaching legendary status.

His running career up until this time, both amateur and professional, had been pretty much free from any major behind-the-scenes problems. He had dealt with the issues with Harry Rosenthal and the amateur unions, but Tom had always remained on good terms with Rosenthal throughout their time together. But a few days after Tom's win in Buffalo, Tom Flanagan abruptly announced that he was leaving Tom to pursue other business interests. Underneath the sudden departure, a personal falling out between Tom and his training staff seemed apparent.

Flanagan's brother Mike, who had been put in charge of Tom's training, was quoted in Toronto newspapers saying, "Longboat is the most contrary piece of furniture I ever had anything to do with." It was terrible timing to have his training staff quit on him since they had set up another race at Madison Square Garden against famed British long-distance runner Alfie Shrubb.

The stakes were high in this race, and for those who picked the right winner, the windfall would be quite profitable, but noted gambler Tom Flanagan simply had had enough of his Native runner. Tom had never believed in any sort of strict training regimen and was known to take long breaks between races and training. Time that Flanagan might have used Tom to promote other events but his runner was continually absent. Finally Flanagan decided not to take it anymore.

"I would give a finger to have him beat Shrubb for Canada's sake," Flanagan told the Toronto press, "but I'll not be on the track or have anything to do with him personally. He can win if he is right and I know it, but I am out of the Indian's game for good." Flanagan had sold Tom's contract to a promoter named Pat Powers for $2000 and simply walked away from the man whom he had stood beside two weeks earlier as the best man at his wedding. It was a tough blow for Tom, but there was no time for sentimentality when he had a race to run.

The press started hyping up the race between Shrubb and Tom weeks in advance. Daily accounts of the runners' training and daily routines appeared in newspapers in Canada, the United States and the United Kingdom. If there had been television at the time, it would have surely been one of the most covered sports events to watch. Trains were diverted and schedules changed to accommodate the crowds expected to descend on New York for the race. It was billed as the race of the century.

Alfie Shrubb did not appear out of nowhere. He had long been winning races and setting records in his native England where he was known as the best long-distance runner in the country. Unlike Tom, however, Shrubb had not always been a runner. Having worked as a stone mason much of his life, Shrubb only discovered competitive running at the age of 18. But all those years spent pounding, grinding and shaping stone had given him a trim but well-built physique. Being British, he also possessed a very methodical training style that he stubbornly stuck to, and he was known to train as hard as he ran competitive races. Shrubb would have raced alongside Tom at the 1908 Olympics in London, but as had happened to Tom, Shrubb had been investigated by the Amateur Unions and been found guilty of taking a little too many incentives for his running. Instead of running in the Olympics, Shrubb made the transAtlantic journey to Toronto and competed in a series of professional races around the East Coast against any and all challengers. And like the record of a professional boxer, Shrubb tallied an impressive number of victories with few losses. In 1907 he looked around the racing world for his next and greatest challenge, and his eyes set squarely on one Tom Longboat.

But in 1907, Tom was still considered an amateur, and despite the repeated requests for a race to decide once and for all who was the greatest runner, Shrubb had to wait. Finally on February 6, 1909, Shrubb got his chance to compete against Tom. For this race, Tom had to make sure he was in peak physical condition, but from the outset things did not go in his favour.

In the span of a few weeks, Tom had run two gruelling marathons against the Italian Dorando Pietri. Tom had run himself to near exhaustion in those races, barely crossing the finish line standing up. He had blistered his feet, cut his knee, and surely was suffering a general overall mental drain from the constant running. The training was going badly, and the added pressure of the media coverage brought Tom close to quitting the race in New York completely. He became so concerned about the race that it prompted him to write a letter to his friend Tim O'Rourke. The letter read:

Dear Friend,

Just a few lines to let you know I am not in shape for this race, so I am just thinking of quitting the race before it gets too late. I think the next race puts me out of business… I wouldn't bet a cent if I were you. I'm good for nothing now.

However, Tim O'Rourke was not such a good friend after all, because the letter ended up in the hands of the *Toronto Star* and became front-page news. Tom was incensed at the betrayal and decided that the only way to combat the negative press was to run. It might have helped Tom to know that Shrubb had never run a marathon, or any race over 15 miles (24 kilometres) for that matter, and that he had lost all three of the 15-mile events he had competed in. At the time, oddsmakers were betting heavily in favour of Shrubb after the publication of the letter, but when Tom travelled to Washington, DC, and ran 15 miles in an exhibition run, the prevailing attitudes towards Tom changed overnight. The Tom Longboat everyone knew was back, and on the night of February 6, he showed up at Madison Square Garden in good form, ready for his next challenge.

Before a crowd of 12,000 eager fans, the two runners took their mark on the starting line. Shrubb wore a dark blue tank top with the Union Jack proudly stitched on front, his hair was parted down the middle and pasted to his head, his moustache was trim and proper, his shorts were pure white, and his socks were perfectly knee high. Tom wore a white tank top with a maple leaf emblazoned on the front with matching white shorts, and his hair, while parted down the middle, did not stick to his head, and his socks were not exactly knee high. Uniformed police officers lined the outside of the track to keep the capacity crowd at bay. The runners took their marks, and the crowd cheered with excitement.

At 9:00 PM exactly, the referee's arm went up and fired the starter's pistol. Shrubb took off from the line in characteristic fashion, taking an early lead. Tom had seen this type of tactic many times in his races, and he casually fell into an easy rhythm behind Shrubb. The Brit's strategy was to break out at a blistering pace and maintain that rhythm through much of the race to tire Longboat out.

Shrubb realized that he might get tired keeping up this pace, but he hoped that he could put enough distance between him and Tom to finish out the race in first.

By the halfway point of the race, Shrubb had lapped Tom several times, and at one point it looked as though he would cruise to an easy win. Even if Shrubb had slowed his pace considerably, it would still have been tough for Tom to make up the eight-lap difference. The runners' coaches and trainers briefly jumped out onto the track to hand the men a drink of water or offer some words of encouragement, but neither runner seemed to show the tell-tale signs of marathon fatigue, yet.

The crowd lost its collective energy as the fate of the race by all appearances had already been determined. But anyone who knew Tom Longboat knew that he always saved the best for last. Just past the halfway point of the race, Tom made his move. Running at a faster pace now, he came up behind Shrubb, pushing his body forward to pass the Englishman. Shrubb's pride did not want to let Tom go by, and he picked up his pace. But he wasn't fast enough. Tom pulled out in front and set his sights on making up the lost laps.

Those who hadn't been on their feet now stood to cheer on the Canadian runner once the race looked as though it was going to be the event that had received so much attention in the media. For the first half of the race, the pressure had been on Tom to keep pace and not give Shrubb too much of a lead. Now the ball was in Shrubb's court. Would he continue on to win the race of the century, or would he tire and falter like so many of Tom Longboat victims before him? The suspense was palpable throughout Madison Square Garden, and fans back in Toronto waited by the wires for any little bit of news on the race. The fans knew Tom Longboat, and despite everything that was said about him in the papers, they still cheered when he made his move.

When Shrubb stopped to take a drink of water, Tom kept going and made up more ground. When Shrubb slowed down to a walk, Tom made up even more ground. When Shrubb stopped to change his shoes, Tom gained even more. Shrubb was looking more and more tired with each step, and in the final stage of the race, he was alternately walking and running; a sure sign that he was about to run out of steam. With less than a lap remaining between first and last place, Shrubb suddenly veered off the track and fell into his trainer's arms. It was the end of the race for Shrubb.

Tom managed to push past the crowd surrounding Shrubb and crossed the finish line. He was the greatest runner in the world again, but he did not receive the respect he deserved. Upon returning from New York, instead of a parade and thousands of cheering fans, Tom was met solely by his wife and a few reporters. The crowds had already come out earlier to see Tom Flanagan whom the papers gave the real credit for pushing Tom to victory.

"To Flanagan belongs the real credit of winning the race," wrote *Star* reporter Lou Marsh. "He worked like a hero and pulled a man through to victory who had but little real license to win."

It mattered little what the local rags said about him; Tom was more than content to return to his home near Toronto's High Park and to his new wife. After the media insanity of the race in New York and the aftermath in the press, he wanted nothing to do with racing for a while. He stayed at home, did chores around the house and took time to relax, something he had not done in a long while. But now that he had taken the title of number one professional runner in the world, more runners wanted the chance to take that title for themselves, and the list of challengers was long.

Olympic gold medalist American John Hayes proposed a $10,000 race between himself, Tom and Italy's Dorando Pietri. Aboriginal runners Paul Acoose and Fred Simpson both wanted to challenge Tom in a race to decide the best runner of the Six Nations. A marathon runner from Chicago even challenged Tom to a 160-kilometre race with $10,000 up for grabs. With such high purses to be had, one might think Tom would jump at another chance to race, but he held firm to his convictions. His new manager, Pat Powers, even tried to force Tom into competition by requesting that the Department of Indian Affairs make him honour his contract, but the government refused.

While many claimed that Tom was being lazy and disingenuous in relation to his contract with the promoter, Tom had done three marathons in one month, and he needed some time to rest. Pressure continued to mount on the champion, however, and finally he agreed to do one race. Powers organized a six-man marathon at the New York Polo Grounds on April 3, 1909. Tom would be up against John Hayes, Dorando Pietri, U.S. Amateur Champion Matt Maloney, French waiter Henri St. Yves, and his old rival Alfie Shrubb. Tom agreed to enter the race, but he attached certain conditions. The "stupid, lazy Indian" everyone had labelled him as turned out to be quite the businessman. Tom said he would only run if Powers hired a trainer of Tom's choosing, and that at the end of the race, Powers had to sell his contract to the manager Tom chose. Powers would get a chance to make some money on a big race, and both men would not have to deal with each other any longer.

Despite the other well-respected runners in the field, Tom's odds were placed at 8-5. The six runners

STARTING MARATHON 4|3|09

Start of marathon race at New York's Polo Grounds on April 3, 1909, with (left to right) Alfie Shrubb, Dorando Pietri, Henri St. Yves, Tom Longboat, John Hayes and Matt Maloney.

took to the field under a cool April shower and a light wind that did little to dampen the spirits of the some 40,000 spectators who crowded into the grounds to see the best long-distance runners in the world.

Unlike most of the other events Tom had entered, this one started with a subdued pace, all runners seemingly saving their energy reserves for the final stages of the race. Longboat kept up a decent pace that had him among the leaders by the halfway point of the race, but since he had run so many

Italy's Dorando Pietri takes the lead in the April 3, 1909, race followed closely by St.Yves, Shrubb and Longboat; out of frame are Americans Hayes and Maloney.

marathons in the past three months, he was not in the best physical condition and began to fade by the 28th kilometre of the race.

Those in the crowd who had placed significant bets on Tom to win frantically cheered him on, but to no avail. Tom simply did not have enough energy and had to bow out of the race by the 30th kilometre. Alfie Shrubb removed himself from the race not too long after that, and the unknown Frenchman Henri St. Yves went on to win the race.

American Matt Maloney has the track all to himself during the April 3, 1909, marathon race in New York City.

When Tom was winning, everyone was his friend, but when he lost, newspapers printed long articles (more like rants) against him, and they were often peppered with racist undertones. When he won, he was "the strong noble Native runner!" and when he lost, he became "the stubborn, lazy Injun who was his own worst enemy." As always, Tom couldn't care less about what people said, and he returned home to Toronto to his wife. In the meantime, Powers had had enough of Tom Longboat,

Photographer surprises the April 3, 1909, marathon winner Henri St.Yves as he is surrounded by well-wishers. (Dorando Pietri is to the left of the frame)

and he sold his contract for the low price of $700 to Hamilton businessman Sol Mintz.

Sol, like Harry Rosenthal, was more a professional fan of Tom's than an actual sports agent/manager, but Tom liked the businessman's enthusiasm and figured they could work together on furthering his career, and despite a few bumps along the way, the two became fast friends.

Chapter Six

The Coming Storm

UNDER THE MANAGEMENT OF SOL MINTZ, Tom's life finally fell into a steady rhythm. The press still criticized him, and he was always under pressure to win races, but it was nothing like it had been earlier. Tom proved himself to be one of the greatest runners ever, and anything else he did simply paled in comparison. Mintz cared for Tom and only wanted the best for his running career. No longer was he forced to race marathons just weeks apart, and no longer did his manager treat him as a commodity.

Finally, Tom was living the life he had always wanted. He had the money to live comfortably, with enough left over to help pay for the construction of a new home for his mother and other relatives back on the Six Nations Reserve. That isn't to say that

Tom won all the races he entered. Up until his race with Alfie Shrubb in Madison Square Garden, Tom had kept an almost superhuman winning record. But by the middle of 1909, Tom finally began to show signs of fatigue.

In early May 1909, his old rival Alfie Shrubb was again looking for retribution for previous embarrassments and challenged Tom to a 24-kilometre race in Montréal. This distance was much more suited to Shrubb's running style, and he had no trouble in beating Tom, leading the race from the sound of the starter's pistol to the finish line. Tom kept the race exciting for the fans, but he had no chance in catching the determined Shrubb. It was Tom's first race since bowing out of the six-man marathon in New York, and he was beginning to get back into his normal training routine. Despite the loss to Shrubb, Tom was confident again in his running ability.

A few weeks later, Shrubb and Tom were at it again in a 32-kilometre race at Toronto's Island Stadium. Shrubb ran out to an early lead, but in the later stages of the race Tom managed to kick in that famous high gear of his and closed down the lead Shrubb had built. The two men ran side by side for several kilometres before Tom pulled ahead. Shrubb tried to keep up, but in the last 200 metres of the race, the Englishman walked right off the track.

Longboat continued on and added another win to his record.

Over the next few years Tom continued to race across North America, through small towns and big cities, running marathons and doing short runs both indoors and outdoors. He did not win every race, trading victories several times with rival Alfie Shrubb, but he always managed to put on a good show for the crowds that came out to see him.

But as time went on, Tom noticed that the crowds were getting smaller and smaller at each race. Long-distance running as a spectator sport was nearing the end of its life cycle. Tom no longer had a manager like Tom Flanagan who possessed a unique flare for promoting racing to the general public and could make a two-hour race seem like a Super Bowl event. Many people believed the whole racing circuit had seen its peak with the Longboat races between Pietri and Shrubb at New York's Madison Square Garden. But Tom still could draw in the crowds, and his body had not given up yet.

The start of 1910 was both a good and bad year for Tom on the track. Although he won most of the races he entered, he lost two high-profile matches against Dorando Pietri and Alfie Shrubb.

Those were the races that mattered most and drew in the greatest crowds. Tom did not take those losses lightly, however, because they hurt his pocketbook. But in July 1911 he suffered an even greater humiliation away from the track, one that would tarnish his image for the remainder of his career and add a negative to the already damaged image of Native people.

One warm summer night in July on the streets of Toronto, after having a few too many drinks with friends, Tom was arrested for public drunkenness. Police reported that they found an unsteady Tom on the streets, wobbling his way home and smelling of alcohol.

The judge convicted Tom of drunkenness in a public place and gave him a suspended sentence. Despite the judge's good-natured gesture, the public damage had been done, and stories of the "drunk Indian" circulated in the press to the point where Tom was labelled an alcoholic. Nothing was further from the truth.

Granted, he did enjoy a few beers every now and again, but that hardly classified him as an alcoholic. It was almost too hard not to drink sometimes. As a local celebrity, whenever Tom entered a bar, several patrons offered to buy him drinks.

Even if the myths of his great drinking habits were true, Tom surely never would have achieved the level of success in his running career that he had attained. If the roles were reversed and, say, Alfie Shrubb had been arrested for public drunkenness, the papers would have passed off the story as just a talented athlete blowing off a little steam. But for a Native person, one whiff of booze and everyone cries alcoholic. The power of prejudice won over a lot of people, and while he remained a respected and popular hero to many, the allegations of alcoholism never went away.

To show the press and his fans the truth of the matter, one month after the drunkenness incident, Tom entered two races in August, and he had two of the best performances of his entire career.

Both races were held at Hanlan's Point Stadium on the Toronto Islands, with the first event scheduled for August 14, 1911, putting him up against Alfie Shrubb over a track set at 12 miles (19.3 kilometres). Normally this was a distance that Shrubb excelled in and always had success in against Tom. Although Shrubb led much of the race, Tom was never more than a few steps behind his longtime rival. Past the 8-mile marker, Tom inched his way closer and closer to Shrubb, and soon the two men were running shoulder to shoulder.

The crowd in attendance was stunned to see Tom challenging Shrubb so feverishly in what was thought to be a sure win for the Brit. All the negative stories in the press about Tom's public drunkenness seemed to fuel his desire to win the race. Bowing out of the race was not an option for either of the runners.

Both ran a hard-fought race, but in the end it was Tom who pushed through to the finish with a full lap lead on Shrubb. The victory was one of Tom's finest performances. He not only managed to maintain the feverish pace set by Shrubb, but he also beat the plucky Englishman at his own game.

The second 12-mile race took place two weeks later on August 28 against three world-class runners: glutton-for-punishment Alfie Shrubb, Charles Hefferon—a South African who had finished in second place in the marathon during the 1908 London Olympics—and rising star A.E. Wood. Hanlan's Point Stadium on the Toronto Islands was a popular place for people to escape to at the end of a workweek.

Besides the stadium, where everything from lacrosse games to running exhibitions were held, there was also an amusement park with a roller coaster that could be seen from the grand stands of the stadium, large green spaces and cafés. It was on a beautiful summer day that approximately 9000 jammed into the stadium to see the race.

For the first half of the race, the runners jockeyed back and forth for the lead. None of the runners wanted to be the first one to make the break for the finish and waste all their energy early on. Nearing the 10-mile (16-kilometre) mark of the race, Tom and the young A.E. Wood made their move for the lead. The two runners chased each other over the next two miles and built up an insurmountable distance between themselves and Hefferon and Shrubb.

During the last lap, Wood and Tom matched each other step for step. The entire crowd jumped to their feet as the two men's faces showed the strain of trying to suck out the last little bits of energy from their muscles. It was a close race down to the finish, but Tom edged out the newcomer by a stride. Tom got the official time from the referee at 1:02:32.04. It was the fastest 12 miles he had ever run, surprising even himself.

The victory was sweet vindication for his career after the embarrassment suffered over the drinking incident, and the win proved to everyone that Tom Longboat was far from done as a professional runner.

In fact, Tom had been around long enough in the running world that he felt it was time to stop paying someone to run his career, and he decided to take over his own management. He purchased his contract from Sol Mintz and arranged his own races.

Bibliothèque Saint-Claude Library

For the first of his bookings, Tom travelled to Scotland in January 1912 to compete in two races in the city of Edinburgh's Powderhall Stadium. The first race was set for the marathon distance, but things went poorly for the Canadian runner from the start. About halfway through the race, Tom slowed down, favouring his right knee. He tried to walk off the pain, but it got worse, and he was forced to withdraw from the competition.

The sore knee put the remainder of his trip overseas in doubt, because if he could not run, he was useless to the promoters. But Tom managed to get himself back into fighting form, and a month later he was set to race a 15-mile course against some of Europe's greatest long-distance runners.

The other runners could not believe their eyes as Tom simply burned up the track, winning the race in a professional record time of 1:20:04. Tom was a sensation in Europe, and the crowds that came out to see him were proof that people still wanted to see Tom Longboat the runner.

In the three years since making the switch to a professional running career, Tom had done pretty well for himself financially. At a time when the average working-class salary was no more than $600 per year, Tom had accumulated $17,000 over a three-year period. This allowed him to lead a relatively opulent lifestyle for the time. He wore nice

Rival runners (from left to right) Meadows, Wood, Queal and Longboat line up to meet the press on the grass of Ebbets Field, in Brooklyn, New York. The photo is not dated, but the picture might have been taken on the day of, or just prior to, a race on August 9, 1913.

suits, smoked fancy cigars and was known to throw expensive parties at his home. And the money kept rolling in.

For the rest of 1912 Tom was in peak running form and won a majority of the events he entered. Although he was running the most exciting races of his career, long-distance running began to fall out of favour with the public.

The global economy was in recession, and people did not have the dispensable income to pay to see a foot race. Added to that was the fact that organized team sports were quickly becoming the sport of choice for newer generations, with the rise in popularity of baseball, football, and hockey league across North America.

People had already seen Tom run against the likes of Alfie Shrubb and Dorando Pietri plenty of times, and there were not enough new high-profile challengers who could bring in the spectators. Tom Longboat was the greatest long-distance runner alive, but no one seemed to care anymore, and while he tried to figure out a way to get his career back on track, an incident in Europe turned the world's attention to more important matters than foot races.

Chapter Seven

Fog of War

TENSIONS HAD BEEN MOUNTING in Europe for several decades prior to World War I as the various empires jockeyed for power. Dangerous rivalries were created among countries for control over the global colonies, national glory and superior military might. Italy, Austria-Hungary, Germany, United Kingdom, Ottoman Empire and Russia were all involved in the play for power that eventually came to the tipping point. Countries were involved in an arms race that saw the build up weapons that fuelled a war like none the world had seen before. All that was needed was a slight push and Europe would descend into chaos. That push came, when on June 28, 1914, a Bosnian Serb student named Gavrilo Princip took matters into his own hands.

Opposed to the Austro-Hungarian Empire's control over his homeland, Princip became a member of Young Bosnia, a group whose motivation was to support the unification of Southern Slavs and aid in the creation of a Greater Serbia free from the tyranny of the empire. But an independent Greater Serbia was seen as a destabilizing force in the region as the Ottoman Empire, the Austria-Hungarians and the Germans all sought control over the volatile area. The actions taken by Princip in late June of 1914, set in motion a series of events that the world would not recover from until the end of World War II and even well into the 1990s with the war in Bosnia.

On June 28, 1914, General Oskar Potiorek, governor of the Austrian provinces of Bosnia and Herzegovina, invited Austro-Hungarian Empire Archduke Franz Ferdinand and the Countess Sophie to Sarajevo to watch his troops perform various manoeuvres in a display of the empire's power in the region. Ferdinand knew the visit was dangerous because his uncle, Emperor Franz Josef, had been the target of assassination by another separatist group in 1911. But the Archduke insisted on the visit, and just before 10:00 AM on Sunday, Ferdinand and the Countess arrived by train and jumped into a waiting car that was to follow a parade route through town. Lining the route of the parade were seven members from Young Bosnia, including student Gavrilo Princip.

Each one of the members lined up with the full intention of assassinating the Archduke. At 10:15 AM, the car carrying the royals passed in front of the central police station, at which time one of the conspirators tossed a hand grenade at the procession. Seeing the grenade fly through the air, the driver stepped on the gas and rushed the Archduke out of harm's way. But the grenade went off and ended up injuring several bystanders.

Archduke Ferdinand later decided, despite the danger, to visit the injured bystanders in the hospital. In the meantime, Princip had gone to a café, resigned to having failed at his mission, when the hand of fate intervened. Suddenly Princip noticed the Archduke's car drive right by the café, apparently having taken a wrong turn. Realizing his mistake, the driver put the car into reverse, but this caused the engine to stall, leaving the Archduke out in the open with no protection. It gave Princip the perfect opportunity to execute his plan. He approached the car, pulled out his gun, and fatally shot the Archduke and his wife.

The Austro-Hungarian government used the assassinations as a pretext to suppress the Serbia populace with the backing of the German government. The Serbians, supported by Russia, mobilized their forces in response, and on the same day that the Archduke and his wife were killed, Austria-Hungary declared war on Serbia, thereby bringing Germany and Russia into the conflict. Germany had set its sights westward and began plans to move on to Belgium and into France. This brought France into the conflict, and Britain soon followed suit after a promise to help protect French sovereignty. By August 1914, Europe was embroiled in the largest conflict since the Napoleonic Wars. With the United Kingdom fully involved in the war, this meant that all Dominions of the British Empire, including Canada, were now fully committed to a war that began as a European conflict and turned into a world war.

On August 5, 1914, Governor General of Canada Prince Arthur declared war on Germany. Sir Wilfrid Laurier spoke for Canadians when he said, "It is our duty to let Great Britain know and to let the friends and foes of Great Britain know that there is in Canada but one mind and one heart and that all Canadians are behind the Mother Country." Canada was at war, and it soon called on its best and brightest to arms.

At that time, Canada only had a standing army of just over 3000 men and a small navy, but within a matter of a few months, some 35,000 men had flocked to recruiting stations across the country.

In principle, every Canadian citizen and member of the British Empire was welcome to join the fight, but when black Canadians attempted to join the fight, they were initially turned away as were Aboriginal Canadians. In 1915, with the war taking lives at an alarming rate, the Canadian government altered their policy towards the visible minorities and allowed them to enlist.

The total involvement of the country in the war effort greatly affected organized sports. As many young men enlisted in the army, sports teams simply did not have the bodies to continue operating. The same thing happened to the amateur unions and associations across Canada, such as Tom's old Irish Canadian Athletic Club, and many simply folded or suspended operations for the duration of the war. This meant that professional runners like Tom Longboat and Alfie Shrubb no longer had the audience to ply their trade in front of as many of the competitions had been absorbed into the military.

However, not all military sports activities were as commonplace as simple running competitions. In the book *Tom Longboat*, Bruce Kidd notes that on April 14, 1915, an article in the *Manitoba Free Press* reported on the unusual use of a commonplace sports item.

"Canadian troops at the front have discovered a new use for lacrosse sticks, namely throwing of hand grenades into German lines…Over 500 sticks have been purchased to try out the scheme."

Tom for his part put his running career on hold and signed up for military duty in January 1916. At first he joined the proud men of Canada's 37th Haldimand Rifles Battalion and simply began his training. Tom was preparing to go straight through to the front lines when a familiar face entered his life once again. Tom Flanagan and a friend named Dick Greer had recently joined the armed forces as well, forming their own unit, the 180th Battalion. The two men recruited their friends from around Toronto, and since Flanagan knew a lot of people in the sports world, the battalion acquired the new moniker of the 180th Sportsmen's Battalion.

As the officer in charge of the 180th Battalion, Flanagan's first order of business was to transfer Tom from the 37th Battalion. With the famed Tom Longboat on board and the managerial powers of Tom Flanagan, the Sportsmen's Battalion did everything but fight in the first part of the war.

Aboriginals were a large part of the Canadian military war effort during World War I, and although they did not receive the full recognition they most likely deserved, they fought with distinction and honour that made them legendary and sought-after additions to regiments. One such soldier was a Corporal Francis Pegahmagabow of Parry Sound, Ontario. A sniper during the war, Corporal Pegahmagabow won fame by killing 378 enemy soldiers throughout the war, and at the famous battle of Passchendaele, he led his company in the capture of some 300 German soldiers.

But the rigours of military life were not for everyone, and Tom had trouble fitting into the strict rules and regulations of military life. Through much of Tom's life up until that time, he had always remained a free spirit. From the moment he had escaped the Mohawk Institute as a young boy, he knew he was not one to follow orders. And the military hierarchy was based on following orders. Tom had to learn and adapt to the structured life of the military. Fortunately, in his first full year in the military, he and his Sportsmen's Battalion did not have to raise their guns.

Using Tom Flanagan's flare for organizing events, the Sportsmen's Battalion was deployed more as troop entertainment than anything else, and instead of fighting, Tom spent most of his time running. Races were organized in and around the Toronto/Montréal corridor to entertain the troops. Tom, dressed in his battalion's colours, challenged other military men in races of varying distances. He didn't always win the races, but the troops had a good time seeing the famous Tom Longboat in the flesh. But besides racing, Tom also got into his fair share of trouble.

Being such a visible celebrity in the military ensured that Tom was one of the more popular soldiers wherever he went and that often led to trouble. Soldiers often bought the famous runner drinks, leaving people like Tom Flanagan to bail him out of trouble. One incident recorded in Jack Batten's excellent book, *The Man Who Ran Faster than Everyone*, relates a story in which Tom and his fellow soldiers from the 180th were assigned to hold back the crowds while the 75th Battalion boarded the train for the long ride to Halifax and then onto England. In the chaos that ensued, several of the soldiers from the 75th recognized Tom and began pouring him drinks, and they managed to pull him onto the train to continue the party. Tom was so involved in the celebrations that he failed to get off the train. It took Flanagan three days to realize that Tom was in Halifax. As punishment, Tom spent much of his early time in the war scrubbing latrines, peeling potatoes and cleaning mess halls.

He enjoyed his time representing his battalion in running competitions, but military life was too stifling for him, and Tom did not hide the fact that he wanted out. After one race in particular, Tom was presented to His Majesty, King George V of England

and was asked if there was anything he could do for Tom. He replied, "Yes, get me out of here and let me go home to my mother." This was not the way to speak to a royal and definitely not the attitude that a Canadian soldier was supposed to portray. The military finally had enough of Tom's antics, and in order to straighten him out, transferred him to the 3rd Battalion, which got its first taste of action in February 1917.

But rarely did Tom ever pick up a gun in a fight as he was assigned a specific role that perfectly suited his special talents; he was an army runner carrying messages to and from the frontlines. It was a strange twist of irony that Tom the marathon runner had turned into an army messenger, given that the marathon event itself had originated from the story of an army runner who had carried a message from the city of Marathon to Athens.

The job of relaying messages was often used during wartime. In the "fog of war," a special term that captures the uncertainty and confusion that surrounds an engagement or campaign, when all forms of electronic communication has failed, the military brass often turned to the old reliable method of sending messages via courier. Messages needed to be sent between generals and commanders so that attacks and defences could be coordinated. It was not a job for the faint of heart nor a slow runner.

Messengers had to contend with running between firing lines, over ground that always carried the threat of land mines, bombardment of enemy guns, shells and, of course, bullets.

The natural enemy of the army runner was the sniper. Snipers loved to pick off the runners because of the special challenge of a moving target. It appeared that Tom was a difficult target to hit, because he went through most of the war without suffering as much as a scratch. But that is not to say he didn't have any close calls. When Tom was interviewed after the war, he said that the first time he heard a shell whiz over his head, "I never thought I'd see Canada again."

One of the stories that surfaced out of the war was that Tom and some other soldiers were buried in the muddy ground for six whole days when a shell exploded nearby and sent a wave of earth crashing down upon them. The newspapers ran with the story that had Tom lying under mounds of muddied earth for six days, fighting off rats and staying quiet so as to avoid German detection. But in an interview conducted after the war, Tom put that rumour to rest when he told the Toronto papers he had just gotten splattered with mud and knocked down when a shell exploded near him. But the admission did not stop the story from being printed over and over again in the press. The country needed its heroes, and Tom was more than happy to oblige.

In between battles, Tom was back on the track, running in competitions against his Canadian brothers in arms. But when duty called, Tom served his country with honour and pride. Probably the most dangerous engagement Tom fought in were the famous Canadian battles of Vimy Ridge and Passchendaele.

The Battle of Vimy Ridge has become a symbol of the Canadian sacrifices made during the war and is often said to have been a defining moment in our collective history. The objective of the engagement was to take control of the German-held high ground at the northernmost end of the British-led Battle of Arras. Gaining control of this ground meant that the British southern flank could advance without being outflanked by the German army. From April 9 to April 12, 1917, the Canadian Corps combined technical and tactical innovations that had the Germans on the defensive the entire time. The Canadian forces meticulously planned the attack that was supported by powerful artillery and a group of some of Canada best trained soldiers, among them Tom Longboat.

During the peak in fighting, it was Tom's job to run through a landscape torn up by constant bombardment, through mud that could swallow a man alive, through shifting trench lines filled with diseased water and rats, to get his messages to the high command. Most of the time he had no idea if the Canadian soldiers he needed to deliver the messages to were alive or dead. Sometimes in the chaos of the war, he didn't even know if he would be running into a German or Canadian trench; the lines were that close.

The cross-country running was something Tom was used to from his days on the reserve, but this countryside had bullets, bombs, barbed wire and enemy soldiers trying to kill him. Often when a fog rolled in off the ocean, Tom could not see two feet out in front of him and sometimes was forced to lie in wet trenches for the weather to clear or else he risked being caught behind enemy lines. The constant running put a strain on his back, a condition that remained with him after the war ended.

In Passchendaele, Tom again served bravely under some of the most horrific of conditions. Led by the British Army, the Battle of Passchendaele involved troops from Canada, Australia, New Zealand, South Africa and France. The intent was to deliver a decisive blow to the German military machine by cutting off their access to the sea and inflicting severe damage to their infantry. Starting in June 1917, the British forces tried on many occasions to break the German line, but the infantry was too well entrenched, and with each push forward, the Brits were forced back under heavy fire.

The battle has become synonymous with the misery of fighting in the thick mud and water of World War I. Soldiers told stories of lying in trenches for days on end, ankle to waist deep in mud and water as bullets flew overhead. The constant whizzing sound of artillery shells made grown men cry and call out for their mothers in the middle of the night. Pictures of the battlefield show soldiers mired deep in a post-apocalyptic wasteland of exploded trees, fields of barbed wire, landmines and miniature lakes, created when shells landed and subsequently filled the holes with water. The battlefield became a patchwork of muddy trenches, wooden walkways and bombed-out plains. It was not uncommon to hear stories of soldiers simply drowning in the mud. Hell had been brought to earth, and Tom Longboat had to run through it all.

When the British Army continued to fail in their attack, their divisions at the battle for the town of Passchendaele were replaced by four divisions of the Canadian Corps on October 18, 1917. The 3rd Canadian division, of which Tom was a member, was up at the frontlines of the battle as they pushed their way through the German defences, Tom all the while running messages back and forth to the army command. In the 16 days that the four divisions of the Canadian corps were involved in the fight, they suffered 15,654 causalities with over 4000 dead. Tom Longboat was one of the lucky ones who survived.

In the fog of war, ambiguity is present in the structure, strength, capability and disposition of a soldier's own and adversarial offensive and defensive assets. Not knowing the strengths or weaknesses of your own army can be caused by a failure to report material deficiencies or an unwillingness to escalate concerns, leading to a false view of the battlefield that can result in unwanted problems—for example, friendly fire incidents, troop shortages on attack and false information flowing between different levels of command. It was part of Tom's job as an army runner to combat the fog of war that was always trying to subvert the military effort. But in the end Tom himself became one of its victims.

Back home in Toronto, Tom's wife Lauretta nervously waited for any news from her husband. A letter, postcard or a simple memento sent in the mail that would let her know her husband was alive. As difficult as the war was for the men on the frontlines, it was just as hard for their loved ones at home, as each day news of the increasing casualties rolled in from the presses. Each phone call made Lauretta jump, and every time someone knocked on her door she felt her heart sink. Was it a letter telling her Tom had been killed in action, or was it a letter from him telling her how much he loved her? Unfortunately, on more than one occasion, Lauretta received a letter from the Canadian military telling her that Tom had been killed in action.

This was not an uncommon occurrence during the war. Frequently, if a soldier missed a roll count or was transferred to another unit and the proper paper work was not filed, it often led to a letter being automatically sent out. This happened to hundreds of Canadian soldiers whom the military simply lost track of and labelled as killed in action. The second time this happened to Lauretta and she did not hear from her husband, she took him for dead.

But as crushing as this news was to Lauretta, according to Tom's son, Tom Longboat Jr., she married another man. "There was a rumour he had been killed in action. When he got home, he found out his wife had married another man. He was pretty mad, he could have killed her I guess, but people told him not to bother about her. So he went with my mother."

Tom spent the remainder of the war running messages and running races. In 1919, when the war came to an end, he could finally stop running and return home to Canada. When he came back though, he did not have a loving wife waiting for him at Toronto's Union Station; instead he filed for divorce.

But Tom was a handsome and famous man, and he did not have to wait long before a woman named Martha Silversmith came into his life. A Seneca from the Six Nations Reserve, Martha was completely different from Tom's former wife. Martha was the same age as Tom and was a soft-spoken woman. She may not have had the same beauty as Lauretta, but she suited Tom's personality much better. The couple married in 1920 and had four children together.

Before starting his new marriage and settling down with a steady job, Tom had a few more races left in his legs, but the racing scene had all but withered away, replaced by team sports such as hockey and baseball. The last great race of his career came at the tail end of his service in the military, on the night of July 18, 1919, at the very familiar Halan Point Stadium on the Toronto Islands.

The event was called the Grand Army of Canada Show, meant to celebrate the achievements and sacrifices of those brave Canadians who had fought in the war. While there were a lot of military personnel and their families in attendance, a significant number of the general public turned out to see the legendary Tom Longboat run one more race. Some 4000 people turned out to watch a three-mile race between Tom and an old opponent from the pre-war days, American Billy Queal.

Once again the crowds at the race cheered the name of Tom Longboat as he approached the starting line. At the age of 32, Tom was still in top marathon shape, ready to teach any challenger that he had what it took to be number one.

When the pistol sounded, Tom was the one who broke out to the early lead. Because the race course was short, Tom thought he could burn off the extra reserves that had always seen him through in his earlier long-distance races.

The strategy appeared to work as he had a comfortable lead on Queal coming into the last stage of the race, but the younger American was able to push through and close the gap. Tom stared straight ahead at the finish line and was shocked to see the American suddenly pull out ahead of him, even though only a few hundred metres were left to go.

The two men broke their pace and sprinted to the finish. They ran neck and neck towards the finish line, but Tom was not going to succumb to the upstart American in front of his home crowd. He managed somehow to give one more push, and he beat Queal to the line just a fraction of a second ahead.

As the crowd leapt to its feet to salute their hero, Tom's soldier friends swarmed him and congratulated him on a job well done. He might have been a running veteran, but he certainly was not washed up. That was the last time people saw Tom Longboat the runner in action.

Chapter Eight

Tom Longboat the Man

THE TIME IN CANADA after World War I was one of great change. The sense of pride and determination that sent many men to enlist to fight against the force of tyranny in Europe was brought back to their native lands and caused a social revolution. In this period of upheaval, Canadian Aboriginals called for their own changes. The one significant demand that Aboriginals called for was to receive the right to vote. Hundreds of Aboriginal soldiers had risked their lives in defence of democracy and their country, and they rightly felt they deserved representation. But their repeated pleas went unheard, and the Native people of Canada did not get the right to vote until 1960.

With rising inflation, increases in the cost of living and many factories closing down after the war, returning Canadian soldiers were left without work, including Tom Longboat. Although he ran in a handful of exhibition races, the professional circuit had dried up. As well, Tom had recurring back and knee problems that kept him off the track for good.

After living in the Toronto area for 32 years, Tom decided it was time to take his new bride and travel out west for work. He tried to take advantage of a program the federal government had set up for returning soldiers that gave them a land grant to start up a farm. This was Tom's only hope for a source of income, since the money he had earned from his years of competitive running had all but disappeared.

During all his years as a professional runner, Tom had never saved any of his hard-earned money. He had come from the poverty of the reserve, and the sudden wealth he attained was a difficult responsibility for a young man. Instead of investing his money, Tom spent it on stylish clothes, bowler hats and fancy leather shoes. By the early 1920s, the only thing left to his name was the house on the reserve that he had built for his mother. The land grant from the federal government would provide Tom with the opportunity to get his finances back in order and allow him to start the family he always wanted.

Tom packed up his meagre belongings, and he and his new wife headed out west. But upon arrival, he found out that his application for the grant had been mishandled in a bureaucratic mistake that prevented him from attaining his grant. Tom moved to the outskirts of Edmonton and later into the city, where he got work as a shipping clerk in a warehouse.

Once settling into their new home, Tom and his wife had four children in quick succession. But Martha never got used to living in the city. She was far away from the familiar land that she loved, far from the family and friends that she had grown up around, and she generally disliked the idea of raising her family in the conservative west. Their first child, born in 1921, was a daughter named Phyllis; Teddy followed soon after in 1923; then Tom Jr. in 1925; and finally Clifford in 1927. Soon after the birth of Phyllis, Tom agreed to move back east in October 1922.

Back in Toronto, Martha might have been happy in her familiar surroundings, but Tom was out of work, and the family was broke. With nowhere else to turn, Tom enlisted the help of his old friend Tom Flanagan. Flanagan was more than happy to place a call to a business acquaintance of his at the Dunlop Rubber Company in west Toronto where Tom landed a job as a general labourer. He earned just three dollars per day, considerably less than what he used to bring in as a professional runner, but his wages put food on the table and a roof over his growing family. Little did he know that a day would come where his job would put all that he had worked for in jeopardy.

While working in the warehouse of the Rubber Company, Longboat was going about his daily routine of helping out wherever he could when he turned down the wrong aisle where some co-workers were adjusting large pieces of rubber on high stacks. One stack fell and dropped onto Tom's left foot, crushing one of his toes. Doctors told him he had to have his toe amputated. It was tough to hear, but Tom did not accept the doctor's recommendation. After all, what did this doctor of the white man's medicine know? Tom had never accepted his ex-wife's religion and had always kept his connection to his Native culture. He went back to the reserve to get a second opinion from the man who acted as the Six Nations' medicine man. The medicine man mixed together a bunch of herbs into a potion that he applied to Tom's injured foot. When the bandage was removed three weeks later, Tom's toe had completely healed.

In the meantime, the Dunlop Rubber Company job had run its course, and Tom caught onto a job in Hamilton working in local steel mill. Again Tom moved his family but was forced to return to Toronto after the failing economy caused the steel company to make cutbacks. Tom was then lucky enough to find work as a City of Toronto employee working in the Street Cleaning Department. It wasn't the type of job Tom had envisioned for himself, but in the tough economic times of the late 1920s and early 1930s, he was just happy to be working.

He worked for the city as a teamster then became a garbage man. Tom never saw his position as demeaning, and he was a big part of the community in which he did his work. Although it was simple work, it paid for a nice house in a good neighbourhood, his kids all went to school, and the family had enough money to throw the occasional party for friends.

In 1927, he was invited to participate in a four-mile race to celebrate Hamilton's Diamond Jubilee. Organizers of the event invited several of Canada's most famous running legends, including William Sherring (winner of the 1906 Olympic marathon gold medal), Eddie Cotter (a former winner of the Around the Bay Race in Hamilton), and of course Tom Longboat. When Tom's name was called over the speaker, the crowd burst into applause, instantly recognizing the running legend. Tom led the whole race, and for his effort he got to take home his first car. All his life he had used his own two feet to take him places, and now he could relax behind the wheel of his new car. After that he often went on trips back to the reserve with his family and around the various lakes and resorts of southern Ontario.

Each year he returned to the Around the Bay Race as their official spokesperson and celebrity official, handing out prizes and shaking hands. He often made special appearance at fairs and annual runs and was more than happy to oblige, but after one exhibition in particular, his life took a turn for the worse.

In 1932, after making an appearance at the Canadian National Exhibition, where he shook hands and signed autographs, Tom left the Exhibition with his family and stopped by a local radio station to do a quick interview while his family waited in the car. When he finished his interview, his youngest son, five-year-old Clifford, ran out into the street to greet his dad, only to get hit by a passing car. His son was declared dead upon arrival at a local hospital. It was the saddest day of Tom's life, and he never fully recovered from Clifford's death.

Now in his early 40s, despite the tragedy of losing his son, Tom continued to accept invitations to running exhibitions around the Toronto area. In 1931, he even met up with his old rival Alfie Shrubb for a race. Although the runners lacked the energy of youth, the crowds still cheered for them like the crowds had done 20 years earlier.

Apart from taking part in the occasional race, Tom's life continued pretty much uninterrupted, and he gradually drifted out of the public con-science, until 1937 when a *Globe and Mail* reporter tracked down the old athlete and wrote an article on him.

Youngsters in North Toronto are fired with a new ambition, not merely to be engine drivers, G-men or even cowboys. Their growing goal now is to be a street cleaner. That is what their idol is—a man who 30 years ago was the most famous athlete in the world and the idol of Canada... "Oh, I'm not news any more," protested the once famous marathoner when a reporter discovered him sweeping leaves on Lawrence Avenue. "I've had my day—and no regrets."

"You're a pretty important fellow to the children of this district," answered the reporter.

"Well, I'm glad they like me," smiled the big Onon-daga Indian. "Maybe all I'm good for now is sweep-ing leaves, but if I can help the kids and show them how to be good runners and how to live a clean life, I'm satisfied."

With a pressure of a bad back, but having a good pension, Tom retired from his City of Toronto job and moved back to the Six Nations Reserve with his wife to a small house. Life settled down to a steady rhythm of long walks and conversations with old friends. His children had gone on to their own lives, and his two sons followed in their father's footsteps joining the Canadian military and seeing action in World War II.

However, Tom did have time to take on one last crusade. Throughout his life he was dogged by allegations of alcoholism. It was true that he did occasionally drink a few too many beers but no more than the next man. During most of his glory days he had heard rumours of a man pretending to be Tom Longboat and using that resemblance to get free drinks out of admirers in Toronto and in the Hamilton area. Tom wrote a letter to the *Hamilton Spectator* to put an end to the imposter's free ride.

"This man has been capitalizing on my famous name for the last fifteen or twenty years and I think it's high time I put a stop to it once and for all."

Local media outlets picked up on the letter, and the hunt began for the drunk passing himself off as Tom Longboat. Once the man was found and shut down, Tom could finally clear his name. That part of his life was over.

Time soon began to take its toll on the old runner. Diabetes had now robbed him of his long walks and kept him confined close to home. By 1948, now

60 years old, Tom developed a case of pneumonia that put him in the hospital. Tom spent the New Year in the hospital bed and nine days later succumbed to the pneumonia. On January 9, 1949, at the age of 61, Tom Longboat stopped running.

His death was reported in the local news but nothing to the magnitude that one might expect for an athlete that had once captured the world's attention. At his funeral, a few of his friends from the old running days stopped in to pay their respects—William Sherring, and his old manager Sol Mintz—but the ceremony, held in a traditional Onondaga longhouse, consisted mostly of Six Nations well-wishers. Tom was buried in the traditional Onondaga way, in simple clothing hand-stitched by the women of the village, and he was placed in a simple coffin with a notch cut into one end to allow his spirit to escape.

As for Tom Longboat's material legacy, it was quite sparse. Having lived through both World Wars and the Depression, Tom had to sell off the many medals and trophies that he accumulated over the decades. The few that were left behind were eventually sold for scrap metal. Only four remain for the viewing public to see at the Woodland Cultural Centre on the Six Nations Reserve.

While he may have faded into obscurity later in life, his modest life belied the truth of a man who was once hailed as the fastest human on the earth. Although he had shown the world that he was the best runner alive, he was never able to fully embrace the fame and fortune that was his claim because of the way he looked. During his entire running career, Tom was dogged by the racism that pervaded society. It was a sad fact of life that Tom had to deal with, but he managed to make his way in a white man's world and stay true to who he was and where he came from.

The following is the obituary for Tom Longboat that appeared in a Toronto paper:

> *Although he had been baptized so he could marry in a church, he had kept to the longhouse religion all his life. His god was still the Great Spirit, and he was buried according to the traditional faith. He was dressed in new cotton and wool, which had been hand stitched by the women in his family... On his feet were new buckskin moccasins. A friend whittled a V in the top of the coffin to permit his spirit to escape. The entire service was spoken in Onondaga, the chants led by his two sons.*

Historical Timeline

1784

Establishment of the Six Nations Reserve.

1870s

Canadian government establishes a program to aid in the education of Native peoples.

June 4, 1887

Thomas Charles Longboat is born on the Six Nations Reserve in Ontario. His parents George and Betty Longboat give their son the Onondaga name of Cogwagee, which means "everything."

1892

George Longboat, father of Tom, dies.

1894

Founding of the Hamilton Around the Bay Race.

1896

First modern Olympics take place in Athens, Greece.

1897

First running of the Boston Marathon.

1899

Canadian government places Tom in the Mohawk Institute, an Anglican mission school for Aboriginals in Brantford, Ontario.

1900

Tom illegally leaves the Mohawk Institute.

1901

Bill Davis, a Mohawk from Ohsweken Reserve, comes in second in the Boston Marathon.

1904?

Likely meets Bill Davis, who inspires him to take up a competitive running.

1905

Enters first competitive race—the Victoria Day race near Caledonia, Ontario, and comes in second.

1906

Canadian William Sherring wins the Olympic gold in the marathon event.

1906

Enters and wins *Hamilton Herald* Around the Bay Race. Meets Harry Rosenthal who becomes his first manager.

1906

Harry Rosenthal relocates Tom to Toronto.

1906

Competes in two more races, the Ward Marathon and a Christmas Day Race, and wins both.

February 11, 1907

Competes in first head-to-head and indoor race in Buffalo, New York, against George Bonhag. Tom loses the race.

1907

Leaves Harry Rosenthal as manager and signs up with Toronto's West End YMCA.

1907

Enters and wins the Boston Marathon in a time of 2:24:25, five minutes faster than the previous record. Returns to Toronto for a parade and gala thrown in his honour.

1907

Leaves the West End YMCA and joins the Irish Canadian Athletic Club where he meets Tom Flanagan, his new manager.

July and August 1907

Competes in two races, one at the Ottawa Carnival, and the other at the Toronto Police Games. In each race, Tom is put up against four runners over a distance of five miles. The other runners change during the race while Tom continues to run. He wins both races.

October 1907

Works in a cigar store, greeting customers and signing autographs.

1907

American Amateur Union bans Tom from any future competition, for accepting money.

1908

Travels to London to compete in the Summer Olympics in the marathon event. Collapses near the end of the race due to heat exhaustion.

1908

Turns professional.

1908

Competes in a marathon race at Madison Square Garden, New York, versus Italian Dorando Pietri. Longboat wins the race.

1908

Marries Lauretta Maracle in the town of Desoronto.

1909

Tom Flanagan quits as manager. Tom's contract is sold to sports promoter Pat Powers.

1909

Competes in what was hailed as the race of the century in Madison Square Garden against Englishman Alfie Shrubb. Over the marathon distance, Longboat wins when Shrubb is forced out due to exhaustion.

1909

Pat Powers sells Longboat's contract to Hamilton businessman Sol Mintz.

1910–13

Participates in a number of exhibition runs and competitions, losing some but winning most.

June 28, 1914

Archduke Franz Ferdinand is shot and killed by Bosnian student Gavrilo Princip, sparking the outbreak of World War I.

1916

Tom enlists in the Canadian Army. For the first year, he spends most of his time in running exhibitions for troops and as part of his regular training.

1917–19

Used as an army runner, sending messages between the frontline and command; is twice declared dead by the army.

1919

Divorces Lauretta Maracle. Retires from professional running but continues through much of his life making appearances at events and running exhibitions.

1920

Marries second wife Martha Silversmith with whom he has four children: Phyllis (1921), Teddy (1923), Tom Jr. (1925) and Clifford (1927–32).

1920

Moves out west to take advantage of a government farm grant but his application is denied.

1922

Returns to Toronto.

1922–27

Works in Toronto, Hamilton and Buffalo at various jobs as a labourer.

1927

Gets employment with the City of Toronto's street cleaning department where he works until 1944.

1929

Stock market crash and the beginning of the Great Depression.

1931

Runs in exhibition match against old rival Alfie Shrubb.

1932

Son Clifford, aged five, dies in a car accident while crossing the street.

1939

Outbreak of World War II—both of Tom's remaining sons serve in the war and return home.

1944

Retires from City of Toronto job and moves back onto Six Nations Reserve.

January 9, 1949

Dies in hospital after contracting pneumonia.

Notes on Sources

Books

Batten, Jack. *The Man Who Ran Faster than Everyone.* Plattsburgh: Tundra Books, 2002.

Derderdian, Tom. *Boston Marathon: The History of the World's Premier Running Event.* Boston: Human Kinetics Publishers, 1996.

Kidd, Bruce. *Tom Longboat.* Markham: Fitzhenry & Whiteside, 2004.

Nabokov, Peter. *Indian Running: Native American History & Tradition.* Salt Lake City: Ancient City Press, 1987.

Oxendine, Joseph B. *American Indian Sports Heritage.* Nebraska: University of Nebraska Press, 1995.

Web Resources

www.aboriginalsportcircle.ca/main/tomlongboatawards.html

www.alfieshrubb.ca/index.php/photo_album/image_full/72

www.archives.cbc.ca/sports/athletics/topics/1341-8011/

www.aroundthebayroadrace.com/history.htm

www.davidblaikie.com/david_blaikie/boston/baa_1907.htm

www.edukits.ca/decoteau/history_timeline.html

www.en.wikipedia.org/wiki/Tom_Longboat

www.geocities.com/Athens/Olympus/3808/TLongboat.html

www.histori.ca/minutes/minute.do?id=14298

www.longboatroadrunners.com/about.html

www.lyngwebhosting.com/lbx/Articles/meeting_tom_longboat.htm

www.ontarioplaques.com/Plaques_ABC/Plaque_Brant03.html

www.sicc.sk.ca/saskindian/a77nov70.htm

www.vac-acc.gc.ca/remembers/sub.cfm?source=history/other/native/longboat

ESCHIA
BOOKS

Here are more titles from
ESCHIA BOOKS...

VICTORIA CALLIHOO
An Amazing Life
by Cora Taylor
This is a biography of the woman who partly inspired Cora Taylor's beloved
Our Canadian Girl character, Angelique. The celebrated children's book
author recounts Victoria Belcourt Callihoo's story, growing up in an Alberta
Métis community almost 150 years ago. Callihoo lived to be over 100 years
old, seeing the Canadian West go from buffalo hunts and Red River carts to
fast food outlets and cars.
$14.95 • ISBN: 978-0-9810942-4-3 • 5.25" x 8.25" • 192 pages

WATISHKA WARRIORS
by Daniel Auger
After living in the city for years, Sandy Lafonde returns to her childhood
home at Watishka Lake First Nation to care for her ailing aunt. Little has
changed since she left—a young teen has just committed suicide, a local gang
menaces the area, the community is splintered and dysfunctional, and the
youth are left restless and frustrated.
Sandy feels the need to do something for her community, so she proposes to
start a junior hockey team. At first she is met with resistance, first from the
band council and then from the team itself, who can barely stop fighting long
enough to play hockey. Drawing on her own past, Sandy steps in as coach and
tries to rein in the star player, hot-headed Sheldon Lambert, a 15-year-old
hockey prodigy who just can't seem to stay out of trouble. Sandy struggles to
keep the team and the community together despite crippling odds and the
ever-present gang lurking in the background. And Sheldon faces decisions
that could affect the fate of the team, and his own life.
$14.95 • ISBN: 978-0-9810942-2-9 • 5.25" x 8.25" • 168 pages

FIRST NATIONS HOCKEY PLAYERS
by Will Cardinal
This book features many First Nations hockey players who made it to the
National Hockey League. Among them is Sandy Lake Cree member Fred
Saskamoose of the Chicago Blackhawks, the first Native to play in the NHL.
It also tells the stories of such players as Jonathan Cheechoo, Carey Price,
Sheldon Souray, Jordin Tootoo, Bryan Trottier, Reggie Leach, Stan Jonathan,
Theoren Fleury and Grant Fuhr.
$14.95 • ISBN: 978-0-9810942-1-2 • 5.25" x 8.25" • 176 pages